FIXING THE 401(k)

FIXING THE 401(k)

What Fiduciaries Must Know (And Do) To Help Employees Retire Successfully

Joshua P. Itzoe, CFP®, AIF®

Mill City Press

Mill City Press, Inc.
212 3rd Avenue North, Suite 570
Minneapolis, MN 55401
612.455.2294
www.millcitypress.net

ISBN - 978-1-934937-17-4
ISBN - 1-934937-17-7
LCCN - 2008933889

Cover Design and Typeset by Tiffany Laschinger

Printed in the United States of America

TABLE OF CONTENTS

ACKNOWLEDGEMENTS

First and foremost I would like to thank my wonderful wife Jessica, my son Caleb and soon-to-arrive baby number two (either Ethan or Lydia.) Your love, patience, and encouragement during late nights and long weekends of writing made this book possible. I dedicate it to you.

I would also like to thank my dear friend and business partner, Pat Collins, who offered me great encouragement and insight throughout the writing process. I could not ask for a better person to build a company with.

I owe a great debt of gratitude to both Pete Swisher of Unified Trust and Matt Hutcheson of Matthew D. Hutcheson, LLC. Each of you has been a valuable resource for me on fiduciary matters and has inspired me to become a more effective and knowledgeable fiduciary. In particular, Pete's book *401(k) Fiduciary Governance: An Advisor's Guide* has been an immensely helpful resource and should be required reading for any advisor who deals with 401(k) plans. I appreciate the time you both have spent making this book better through your insights (and critiques).

I would also like to thank several colleagues and friends who provided excellent feedback and support throughout this project, including: John Paliga from Thomas & Libowitz, Jennifer Downs from Benefit Audit Group, Michele Kocak from Independent Benefit Services, Rick Meigs of www.401khelpcenter.com, Irene Catlin and Nicholas Balcken from Greenspring Wealth Management, and Rick Faint from The Cornerstone Professional Group. Thank you for helping make this book become a reality. I'd also like to thank Dr. Marc Baldwin and his staff for their excellent editing services.

Finally, I would like to thank our clients for allowing me to have a job that I am both challenged by and passionate about.

FOREWORD by Matthew D. Hutcheson

You are a fiduciary. With that great responsibility, you literally have the power to improve or impair an individual's quality of life during retirement. That power is why courts have called fiduciary duty "the highest known to the law." It really is that important.

American workers who participate in 401(k) or "401(k) like" retirement plans are not being adequately protected – but easily could be. Currently, plan decision-makers, whether plan sponsors or participants, have few helpful ways to learn – much less understand – the responsibilities, obligations, duties, and actions they must take to properly discharge their fiduciary duties.

It's not your fault. The 401(k) industry has made it difficult to be a good fiduciary. If all fiduciaries understood how easy it actually was to properly discharge their duties, the entire 401(k) landscape would look much different than it does today. Knowledgeable fiduciaries would simply make better (and different) decisions that positively impact outcomes for plan participants.

The book you hold in your hands will change your life forever. If you read it carefully, and deeply consider the message it conveys, you will become that knowledgeable fiduciary; an empowered decision maker that knows what decisions to make, and why a particular decision is being made in lieu of another.

This book will help you discharge your duties *solely in the interest* of plan participants *and beneficiaries* for the *exclusive purpose* of providing benefits.

Following my congressional testimony on March 6,

2007, I delivered a subsequent statement to Congress in order to further clarify the importance of reforming the retirement plan system:

> *The matter of retirement plan economics is not only about dollars and cents; it's also about developing a growing population of responsible professional parties who embrace correct principles and seek the common good of society. As an independent fiduciary without prejudice, that is precisely the lens through which I see things: The goal is to serve the best interests of nearly fifty million individual plan participants—not the self interests of the financial industry. Therefore, these thoughts and comments are offered to link dollars and cents with principles of fiduciary prudence.*

There are many books about 401(k) plans. There are hundreds of thousands of professionals who want to invest your 401(k) plan assets. Very few of them, unfortunately, embrace a "participant first" approach to delivering retirement plan services. That is what makes this book so special. It is focused on one thing: *Protecting future participant benefits*. The goal of this book is to serve the best interests of nearly fifty million individual plan participants.

I fully endorse and support this book and its ideas. I encourage you to give favorable consideration to its message and to purchase a copy for your friends and colleagues so that they too may understand. You can participate in building and protecting the retirement of your employees, associates, and loved ones like never before.

No person can guarantee specific results, however, as I stated during my 2007 testimony to Congress, "*True prudent fiduciary practices should deliver optimal results. Poor or partial fiduciary practices will deliver suboptimal or even poor results.*" That is a strong belief, and I stand by it. That is why I endorse this book and commend it to you.

PREFACE

My journey into the world of corporate retirement plans began while I was a rookie broker for one of Wall Street's largest and most well-respected brokerage firms. Assuming that I could generate enough interest from my clients or prospects, a retirement plan was one of many financial "products" that I could get paid for selling. The firm had relationships with seven or eight of the better-known retirement plan providers (or vendors) which I could offer to my clients. Every so often a "wholesaler" (i.e., salesperson) from one of the companies would buy the brokers in our office lunch (known as a "lunch and learn") in exchange for pitching us on the merits of his or her company's product. This discussion usually focused on which investments or "money managers" were part of the vendor's 401(k) plan, what the broker's commission structure was (that is, how much we would be paid), and, most importantly, what kind of "sales ideas" were working in the market place. "Sales ideas" were always critical to engaging current or prospective clients in a conversation because these led to sales pitches which ultimately led to actual sales if you had enough of these discussions. One idea that every wholesaler recommended was to contact business owners and mention the phrase "fiduciary responsibility" and the liability associated with it. You see, fear and greed play a large role in the world of financial services, and fiduciary liability was often a good conversation starter.

Most of the other brokers in my office discouraged me from pursuing the retirement plan market because of the long "sales cycle" required to land a plan and the seemingly low commissions that could be earned relative to the sale of other types of products. In the brokerage (or insurance) industry, there is a lot of pressure to generate revenue and to do so quickly. Early on, I was told that the attrition rate in the industry was at least 80 percent and the people who survived were the ones who could prospect and sell in the face of intense rejection. As a rookie, I needed to close business and increase my "production" (that is, revenue). A long sales cycle was not an attractive proposition.

However, there were a small number of brokers I knew who "specialized" in retirement plans which meant this was an area of focus for them. Most were established and had enough revenue to support the investment of time necessary to win retirement plan clients. Generally speaking, the retirement plan was looked at as an entree to the business owner and the other company executives. These types of individuals make excellent private clients which made the time investment tolerable. Even still, the focus was almost always product-driven (which I have found continues today).

Periodically, I would come across these types of opportunities and would try to figure out which retirement plan product was the best fit for the client. Truth be told, as a rookie starting out in the financial services industry, I did not fully comprehend how these plans worked because of the complexity associated with them. Just trying to figure out how the compensation structure worked was a chore, not to mention the myriad of legal rules and overwhelming regulations. During this time, one of my best friends was working at a firm similar to mine, and he and I began to discuss the dream of starting our own firm one day. We even put a business plan together. In October of 2004 our dream became a reality, and the firm opened its doors. We had always agreed that one of the challenges of working in the brokerage industry was the conflicts of interest you faced when it came to getting paid. Since we were generally compensated by third-parties to sell their products and services to our clients, the challenge we ran into was that some paid higher commissions than others. For instance, if one product or company paid a 7 percent commission and another only paid a 1 percent commission, which one should we recommend to our client? To compound the issue, the costs and compensation of products were usually not fully disclosed to clients or not disclosed at all. We felt this put clients at a disadvantage and us in a difficult position.

Our firm began with a very simple premise: we would only accept fees directly from clients and solely for our advice, regardless of what products or services were recommended. To accomplish this goal, the firm was organized as a "pure" Registered Investment Advisor (RIA) as opposed to a Broker-Dealer (B/D). We basically turned our back on a system we believed was conflicted and broken and set against the success of clients, and we've never looked back.

At inception, our firm primarily focused on serving affluent individuals and families by providing wealth management and investment advisory services. Along the way, however, we realized that our approach (direct and fully disclosed fees, fiduciary responsibility, independence, etc.) was especially suited for the retirement plan market, and we started an institutional advisory practice aimed at providing fiduciary governance consulting and investment advisory services to retirement plan fiduciaries. I agreed to lead this practice group for the firm and embarked upon learning as much as I could about the retirement plan industry. I was in for quite a surprise.

I chose the title of this book because it embodies my strong belief that the retirement plan industry (and, therefore, many retirement plans) is broken in many ways. I did not come to this realization immediately. In fact, it took me over a year to really get a handle on all the moving parts within a retirement plan and the sleight-of-hand tricks that often take place to propagate the confusion.

Think about the significance of that point for a moment. If I had trouble understanding the complexities of a retirement plan, imagine the difficulty for someone who does not do this for a living – someone like a plan sponsor or participant. I didn't know what I didn't know, and I made some mistakes. Thankfully, since the retirement plan market does, in fact, have a long "sales cycle," I wasn't able to damage any actual clients!

The first area that I felt was sorely misunderstood and which could help both companies and participants was the area of fiduciary responsibility. For all the talk about its importance, I came across very few people who really grasped this confusing and technical area. This included the vendors I dealt with, other advisors I competed against, and, most importantly, the owners and executives of the companies I called upon who were actually fiduciaries themselves. To compound the issue, I felt like the industry did a poor job in terms of disclosing conflicts of interest, making the job of a fiduciary even more challenging, confusing, and risky.

I quickly came to believe that every decision of consequence about a retirement plan was actually a fiduciary decision, so I determined that I would do everything in my power to develop a considerable base of knowledge. I read everything I could get my hands on that discussed fiduciary matters and spoke to anyone who would talk about the topic. Fortunately, I had the opportunity to search out and meet some extremely knowledgeable and helpful folks who invested considerable time and effort to speed up my learning process. One of the best pieces of advice that I followed was to actually read the Employee Retirement Income Security Act of 1974 (ERISA) which is the law that governs retirement plans. It is amazing how much you can learn when you go straight to the source. Because I had a frame of reference to compare many of the things I was being told, my understanding grew exponentially. Fairly quickly, I began to see that I had a better knowledge of fiduciary issues than most of the people I interacted with on a regular basis. This was both encouraging and scary! Over time, this understanding has been critical in allowing us to effectively counsel our clients on matters regarding their company's retirement plan.

I believe plan fiduciaries must make sound decisions in the following three critically important areas for their participants to benefit substantially in terms of achieving a successful retirement:

1. Effective Plan Design
2. Successful Investment Experiences
3. Cost Containment

This book is a culmination of that basic philosophy and approach which I have developed over the years and that we utilize for our own clients. It is meant for anyone who is considered a retirement plan fiduciary. Like everybody, I have my own biases that I stand behind and that I share in the pages that follow. As you will see, I express strong opinions about how retirement plans should be designed, delivered, paid for, and governed, many of which run counter to the way the retirement plan industry currently operates. Many of these ideas (especially when it comes to fees, compensation, and service providers) are not always popular with a lot of the people who work in the retirement plan arena.

My journey has led me to develop a set of core beliefs which guide and influence how our firm advises and works with plan fiduciaries and participants:

- I believe that companies have a responsibility to do everything they can to help their employees retire successfully.
- I believe that fiduciaries have a duty to become better educated about what is required of them, to do their jobs more effectively, and to hold accountable the people they rely on for "advice".
- I believe good fiduciary decision-making depends upon developing and <u>executing</u> a sound fiduciary governance process.

- I believe the industry makes it far too confusing to determine who is responsible for what and that there should be full and easy-to-understand fee disclosure by every person and/or company who provides services to a plan.
- I believe that far too many service providers talk about the importance of fiduciary responsibility but are unwilling and/or lack the knowledge to effectively serve in this capacity.
- I believe that plan fiduciaries and plan participants are best served by a Registered Investment Advisor (RIA) who is appointed as an ERISA §3(38) "investment manager" due to the high likelihood that most participants will achieve sub-optimal investment experiences.
- I believe that the financial success of most Americans (both current and future) depends to a great degree upon making prudent decisions about the retirement plans that will get them to and through retirement. Unfortunately, my experience leads me to believe that this is not the practice in the vast majority of our country's retirement plans.

All of these ideas (plus others) are discussed in the ensuing chapters.

I hope this book serves as a useful resource to the reader and leads to better decision-making by anyone who has influence over a company-sponsored retirement plan. My primary goal is to provide a high level understanding of how these complex plans work, ways they can be designed and delivered most effectively, as well as the basic responsibilities of an ERISA fiduciary. Finally, I outline some actionable steps fiduciaries can take to gain better visibility into their own plans, to hold their service providers accountable, and to make better decisions on behalf of their participants which should lead to successful retirement outcomes and meaningful benefits. I want to stress that the fiduciary process should come before and drive any product-related decision, rather than vice-versa.

This book is not meant to serve as a deeply technical or comprehensive resource on all components of a 401k plan. Reading it will not turn you into an expert on all fiduciary and/or retirement plan matters by itself. However, it should be a good starting point. I am also not providing legal advice or legal opinions. There is no substitute for professional expertise in these matters, and every plan sponsor would be wise to utilize the combined services of a competent ERISA attorney, CPA, investment advisor, and plan provider as necessary. I have included a Glossary of Terms that explains many of the technical terms and concepts used by industry professionals as well as several appendices that may be helpful. The first usage of each term has been bolded and italicized for convenience.

As a fiduciary, you have a significant responsibility and incredible opportunity to positively impact the retirement experience of your participants. By understanding your duties and following certain best practices, you can increase the likelihood they will have a successful and enjoyable retirement experience. I hope this book helps!

Joshua P. Itzoe, CFP®, AIF®
Greenspring Wealth Management, Inc.
Towson, Maryland
April 2008

CHAPTER 1

The 401(k) Industry is Broken!

s a plan ***fiduciary***, the first thing you must realize is that the ***401(k)*** industry is broken in many ways, and, therefore, it is entirely possible that your plan is broken too.

This does not mean that there are not smart, dedicated, and honorable people or excellent companies throughout the industry – there are. However, the system operates in a way that puts you and, more importantly, your employees, at a great disadvantage. The two biggest issues in the industry are the rampant ***conflicts of interest*** that exist and the lack of easy-to-understand ***fee disclosure.*** This negatively impacts your participants' ability to retire successfully and also puts you at risk as a fiduciary because you are personally liable for the decisions that are made about the plan.

Information is a necessary and valuable resource when it comes to understanding how a retirement plan works. However, information alone is not sufficient for a plan fiduciary. It must be paired with understanding in order to make good decisions for the plan and its participants. The combination of information and understanding is known as prudence, which is highly esteemed in the world of ***ERISA***.[1]

This book will help reveal many of the industry practices which put plan participants and fiduciaries at a disadvantage and will help them understand, among other things:

- The basic fiduciary responsibilities outlined under ERISA (Chapter 3)
- The roles, responsibilities, and motivations of the various people/companies involved in selling and servicing these plans (Chapter 4)
- Which questions to ask and what information to gather in order to uncover and reduce the various fees and expenses associated with 401(k) plans (Chapters 6 and 7)
- How to design a 401(k) plan to deliver successful outcomes (Chapter 8)
- How to help employees use the plan most effectively (Chapters 10, 11, and 12)

Armed with both knowledge and understanding, plan fiduciaries will assume a position of control relative to their service providers, achieve greater clarity into their plans' composition and performance, and make better decisions. While plan participants will primarily benefit from improved decision-making, fiduciaries will be able to sleep better knowing they have discharged their duties in a prudent and effective manner.

Questions to Ask:

1. Am I aware of any conflicts of interest that my service providers may have?
2. How do these conflicts impact the objectivity of their recommendations?
3. Am I confident that I have a clear understanding of all fees in my plan?
4. Is it possible my company's plan is broken and I don't know it?

CHAPTER 2

Focusing on Successful Outcomes

Few people would argue that the definition of retirement is changing in the United States. Gone are the days when a company would reward loyal, long-term employees with a gold watch, a guaranteed pension, and medical benefits in retirement. In fact, most employees fail to remain with one company long enough to even qualify for such a benefit. How workers view retirement is also dramatically changing. The "Golden Years" used to mean several rounds of golf each week and martinis at four o'clock every afternoon. Today, the ***baby boomer generation*** is rewriting the rules of retirement to include activities like starting a new business, volunteering time and talents to non-profit organizations, and even going back to school. At the same time, many would-be retirees are facing the grim reality that they are ill-prepared for retirement and realizing that retirement is not a reality at all.

In past decades, employers took responsibility for providing adequate retirement benefits for their workers by using ***defined benefit*** or ***pension*** programs which were ***"trustee-directed."*** In most cases, these plans achieved their purpose of providing retirement income for three primary reasons. First, a sufficient contribution (based on an actuarial formula) was made on behalf of the employee each year. Second, the money was typically invested by professional money managers who had the discipline and knowledge to manage the assets in a prudent fashion and earned acceptable returns. Third, the company had a vested interest to keep fees low since higher fees reduced returns. Lower returns were expensive because the company had to make larger contributions to the plan to meet the funding requirements. Over the past twenty years, most companies have moved away from defined benefit plans due to the cost to maintain them and embraced 401(k) and ***profit-sharing plans*** (often called ***participant-directed*** plans) as the primary means for retirement saving. As the onus for saving has shifted from employer to employee, this transition has had a profound impact on the state of retirement readiness in our country.

In contrast to the general success of trustee-directed plans, the participant-directed approach has fallen short because of high plan fees combined with employees who have neither made sufficient contributions to these plans nor invested their money in a prudent and disciplined way.

In fact, the Center for Retirement Research at Boston College (CRR) recently completed a study that evaluated household pension wealth and retirement income replacement rates from 1992 to 2004.[1]

Through this period, during which time retirement saving went from predominantly defined benefit plans to mostly defined contribution plans, both average household benefits and income replacement rates decreased. According to the CCR Brief, the average household with a head between 51–56 years old had about $114,000 in pension wealth in 2004 which was 11 percent less than in 1992.

Recently, retirement industry experts, academics, and legislators have collaborated to improve the "user experience" for retirement plan participants. The ***Pension Protection Act of 2006 (PPA)*** represented sweeping changes on how retirement plans are designed and operated. Key provisions utilize ***behavioral finance*** research in an attempt to redesign participant-directed plans to look and feel more like trustee-directed plans. Plan design features such as ***automatic enrollment, automatic deferral increases,*** and ***qualified default investment alternatives (QDIAs)*** all serve as means to increase the probability of successful outcomes for America's retirement plan participants and to provide meaningful retirement benefits. These features will be discussed in detail in Chapter 8.

With today's changing retirement landscape and the passage of the PPA, Congress has developed a blueprint for what it believes is necessary to implement an outcome-focused retirement plan. Prudent plan fiduciaries must take a proactive approach to incorporate these new elements into their plan design.

In the future, it is likely that the main determinant of whether a retirement plan was successful (and if the plan fiduciaries were prudent) will be whether the plan provides for adequate and meaningful benefits for its participants. If plan sponsors have not taken the time to understand these PPA-approved features or considered incorporating them into their plan, now is the time to do so.

Questions To Ask:

1. Is my plan designed and managed to achieve successful outcomes and provide meaningful retirement benefits for my participants?
2. Has our plan incorporated the new plan design features approved by the Pension Protection Act (PPA) of 2006? If not, why not?
3. How prepared are my employees for retirement?
4. What steps can my plan take to help my participants save more money by designing the plan more effectively?

CHAPTER 3

An Overview of Fiduciary Responsibility

While most plan fiduciaries have heard the word "fiduciary," few know whom the term applies to or what responsibilities are required. The ***Employee Benefits Security Administration (EBSA)*** of the Department of Labor (DOL) is responsible for administering and enforcing the provisions of the Employee Retirement Income Security Act (ERISA). This law, created in 1974, provides protections for participants and beneficiaries in employee benefit plans, including access to information, and identifies the standards of conduct under the fiduciary responsibilities specified in the law.

Many people are involved in the successful operation of a retirement plan. Some are specifically identified as fiduciaries, some become fiduciaries based on their actions, and others may act under the direction of a fiduciary. According to ERISA §3(21)(A), a fiduciary is any person(s) (or entities) who:

1. Exercises any discretionary authority or discretionary control respecting management of such plan or exercises any authority or control respecting management or disposition of its assets;
2. Renders investment advice for a fee or other compensation, direct or indirect, with respect to any

moneys or other property of such plan, or has any authority or responsibility to do so;

3. Has any discretionary authority or discretionary responsibility in the administration of such plan.

Plan fiduciaries may include, for example, plan trustees, plan administrators, members of a plan's investment committee, or a service provider. According to ERISA §404(a)(1), a fiduciary has four primary duties and is required to discharge those duties solely in the interest of the participants and beneficiaries. They include:

- A Duty of "Exclusive Purpose"
- A Duty of Prudence
- A Duty to Diversify
- A Duty to Follow Plan Documents (unless inconsistent with ERISA)

Fiduciaries who fail to follow these principles of conduct may be held personally liable to restore any losses to the plan, or to restore any profits made through improper use of plan assets.[1] This liability exposes the fiduciaries' personal assets, home, and business to risk. Plan fiduciaries that are shown to have willfully violated their responsibilities can also be subject to criminal penalties and civil actions by participants.

A Duty of "Exclusive Purpose"[2]

ERISA requires a fiduciary to act for the "exclusive purpose" of providing benefits for plan participants and their beneficiaries which includes defraying reasonable expenses of administering the plan. Every fiduciary decision should be focused on delivering successful outcomes for participants, specifically, helping them accumulate the greatest amount of retirement assets at the lowest cost possible. This duty is the most important fiduciary responsibility from which all other duties emanate.

A more detailed discussion of fees can be found in Chapter 6; however, the Department of Labor has clearly stated that a fiduciary "has a specific obligation to ... ensure that fees and expenses are reasonable in light of the level and quality of services provided."[3] This is an area where many fiduciaries fall short because they do not understand the total costs associated with their plan. Without a clear understanding of the fees paid for each service provided to the plan, a fiduciary has no way of making a determination as to whether these services are reasonable. This represents a breach of responsibility.

Overall, the industry has done a poor job with full and easy to understand fee disclosure, and fiduciaries have failed to become educated and to hold their service providers accountable. Unfortunately, ignorance or lack of understanding about fees is not an acceptable excuse for a fiduciary.

Courts have affirmed that fiduciary obligations are among the "highest known to law"[4] and the fiduciary stands in a special relationship of trust. In fact, "fiduciary" is derived from the Latin word fiducia which means "trust." If a plan fiduciary determines that certain elements of the plan are not benefiting participants, he or she has an obligation to make changes.

Fiduciaries are also required to inform participants and beneficiaries of their rights under the plan and must completely and accurately answer participants' questions about the plan. Under ERISA, information disclosure to participants is very important, and fiduciaries have a responsibility to keep participants informed so that they may make their own reasonable decisions about the plan. A breach of duty can occur when a fiduciary makes false representations regarding employee benefits.

A Duty of Prudence[5]

Prudence serves as the cornerstone of fiduciary responsibility. ERISA requires a fiduciary to act "with the care, skill, prudence, and diligence under the circumstances then prevailing that a prudent man acting in a like capacity and familiar with such matters would use in the conduct of an enterprise of a like character and with like aims." This means a fiduciary is considered to be an "expert" when making decisions about the plan, even if ill-suited to do so. Ignorance is not a viable excuse for a fiduciary. If a fiduciary lacks the necessary time, skill and knowledge, he or she has a right as well as a duty to hire prudent experts who can help them meet their responsibilities.

A Duty to Diversify[6]

A fiduciary has a duty to diversify "the investments of the plan so as to minimize the risk of large losses, unless under the circumstances it is clearly prudent not to do so." For participant-directed plans that choose to comply with section 404(c), ERISA requires a plan to offer a minimum of three different investment alternatives, "each of which has materially different risk and return characteristics" so that participants have the opportunity to adequately diversify their accounts. Unfortunately, research shows that most participants do a poor job of making good investment decisions. This will be further discussed in Chapter 5.

A Duty to Follow Plan Documents (unless inconsistent with ERISA)[7]

A fiduciary has a duty to manage the plan "in accordance with the documents and instruments governing the plan insofar as such documents and instruments are consistent with the provisions" of ERISA. For instance, if the plan document provides for eligibility after six months of service, the plan must provide entry once an employee reaches the required length of time.

Avoiding Prohibited Transactions, Self-Dealing, and Conflicts of Interest

There are five categories of ERISA-specified ***prohibited transactions*** that a fiduciary may not cause the plan to engage in, directly or indirectly, with a ***party in interest***. These prohibited transactions include:[8]

- A sale, exchange, or leasing, of any property between the plan and a party in interest
- Lending of money or other extension of credit between the plan and a party in interest
- Furnishing of goods, services, or facilities between the plan and a party in interest
- Transfer to, or use by or for the benefit of a party in interest, of any assets of the plan
- Causing a plan to acquire and to retain employer securities or employer real property in violation of ERISA

In addition, ERISA prohibits fiduciaries from engaging in various acts of self-dealing or conflicts of interest. A fiduciary may not:

- Deal with plan assets in his own interest or for his own account;
- Act in a transaction involving a plan on behalf of a person whose interests are adverse to the interests of the plan, its participants or beneficiaries;
- Receive any consideration for his own personal account from any person dealing with the plan in connection with any transaction involving the plan's assets.

For example, a prohibited transaction would exist between a plan and its trustee if the plan paid legal fees to the attorneys defending the trustee in a criminal prosecution. A fiduciary could not allow plan assets to invest in a life insurance company's group annuity contract and then have his company receive a commission for making the investment. A plan could not purchase a piece of art as an investment and then use it in the company's place of business because it would benefit the company. Or, a trustee could not allow a plan to loan assets to another company the trustee had control over. All of these examples represent fiduciary breaches.

Not All Fiduciaries are Created Equal under ERISA

In today's regulatory environment the word "***co-fiduciary***" has become a popular buzzword and more service providers are marketing this term as though it has magical powers – in most cases it does not. The term is somewhat misleading. Technically, there are fiduciaries and non-fiduciaries. While hiring a service provider that states they assume "co-fiduciary" responsibility is important, it is necessary to understand what this means in the context of the services being provided to the plan and what benefits are provided.

Not all fiduciaries are created equal under ERISA. Fiduciaries fall into two basic categories: ***named fiduciaries*** and ***functional fiduciaries***. Named fiduciaries are designated as such in the ***plan document*** or other service agreement and are usually responsible for controlling or managing a retirement plan's assets or operations. Functional fiduciaries take on fiduciary status because of their actions.

The plan must provide for one or more named fiduciaries that jointly or severally control and manage the operation and administration of the plan. Each plan must have at least one named fiduciary, and, if plan assets are held in trust, the plan must have at least one trustee. If the plan provides for it, any person or group of persons may serve in more than one fiduciary capacity, including serving both as trustee and plan administrator.

Named fiduciaries include:

- ***Plan Administrator (as defined by ERISA §3(16)(A)):*** The plan administrator is the person specifically designated in the plan document or, in most cases, the plan sponsor. The plan administrator oversees the operation of the plan. This should not be confused with a ***Third-Party Administrator (TPA)*** who serves as a "***contract administrator.***"
- ***Trustee:*** ERISA requires plan assets to be held in trust by one or more trustees. The trustees must either be named in the written documents or be appointed by a named fiduciary. The trustee(s) has the exclusive authority to manage and control the assets of the plan and generally are the owners or executives of the plan sponsor. Directed, or non-discretionary trustees may be appointed to execute upon instructions given by the discretionary trustee. Directed or non-discretionary trustees are generally trust companies.

Many people mistakenly believe that fiduciary responsibility (and thus liability) cannot be delegated. In fact, ***ERISA §3(38)*** identifies the role of ***"investment manager."*** Although common sense would dictate that an investment manager is simply someone who "manages investments," this role (and its qualifications) is specifically identified under ERISA. An investment manager is any fiduciary (other than a trustee or named fiduciary) who:

- Has the power to manage, acquire, or dispose of any plan asset;
- Is a ***registered investment adviser (RIA)*** under the ***Investment Advisers Act of 1940***, a bank or an insurance company;
- Has acknowledged in writing that he is a fiduciary with respect to the plan.

According to ERISA §402(c)(3), a named fiduciary may appoint an investment manager (or managers) to manage any plan assets. When this is done properly, the other fiduciaries are relieved of the responsibility for the manager's investment decisions as long as they have prudently selected the investment manager and continue to monitor its performance. This strategy provides for a real transfer of risk from the named fiduciary to the investment manager and I believe is the best approach for both participants and plan fiduciaries (I address this topic in more detail in Chapter 5). As ERISA attorney Fred Reish points out, in this scenario the investment manager takes on "virtually all of the fiduciary responsibility" with respect to management of plan assets.[9]

Under ERISA, fiduciary status can be acquired even where there is no express appointment or delegation of fiduciary responsibility (as in a named fiduciary.) A person may be considered a "functional fiduciary" based on his or her duties relating to the plan regardless of formal title.

The key determinant of whether a person qualifies as a functional fiduciary is whether that person exercises discretionary authority or control over the administration of an ERISA plan, or its assets (such as by rendering investment advice). A person is a plan fiduciary only "to the extent" that he or she possesses or exercises the requisite discretion and control. Control takes many forms, including that of simple influence. Remember, it's "to the extent" (i.e. to any degree, large or small). As you will see in Chapter 4, understanding the role of different service providers can be difficult. Many companies (and individuals) assist plan sponsors concerning plan investment options and go by a variety of different titles that can be quite confusing (broker, registered representative, consultant, financial advisor, etc.) While some of these people serve as fiduciaries, many act in a ***non-fiduciary*** capacity. Others claim not to be fiduciaries but exercise a great level of control or influence over a plan and are thus fiduciaries anyway. Caution: as more service providers use the "co-fiduciary" buzzword to promote themselves, it is important for plan sponsors to understand exactly what this means. There are many different types of co-fiduciary services that vendors offer, and some will promote their "co-fiduciary" status as though it has the ability to transfer or eliminate fiduciary liability. In many cases, it does not. As W. Scott Simon has pointed out, investment consultants come in three basic types when it comes to acknowledging their fiduciary responsibilities under ERISA:

1. those that do not acknowledge any fiduciary responsibility at all,
2. those that acknowledge fiduciary responsibility as a "co-fiduciary," and
3. those that acknowledge fiduciary responsibility as an ERISA §3(38) "investment manager" and §405(d)(1) "independent fiduciary."[10]

As Simon explains, "there are significant differences among such non-fiduciaries and fiduciaries, and those differences can have a direct bearing on the retirement lifestyles of participants in 401(k) plans. Plan fiduciaries must have a good understanding of such differences so that they can protect plan participants and their beneficiaries from the worst of the investment consultants and help them benefit from the services of the best consultants."[11]

Co-Fiduciary Liability

"Co-fiduciary" is fast becoming a popular marketing term in the world of retirement plans. The only reference to "co-fiduciary" in the law is addressed in ERISA §405 which outlines the co-fiduciary liability provisions. As pension expert Pete Swisher clearly states, "a co-fiduciary is nothing more than a fellow fiduciary. In order to be a co-fiduciary, one must first be a fiduciary – there is no such thing as a distinct co-fiduciary status that is somehow different from being a 'true' fiduciary as it is sometimes described."[13] The impact of co-fiduciary liability means that a fiduciary may be held responsible for breaches or mistakes committed by another fiduciary. Co-fiduciary liability is a complex topic that cannot be completely covered in this text. However, ERISA §405(a) does specify three circumstances that give rise to liability:

1. if he participates knowingly in, or knowingly undertakes to conceal, an act or omission of such other fiduciary, knowing such act or omission is a breach;
2. if, by his failure to comply with section 1104(a)(1) of this title in the administration of his specific responsibilities which give rise to his status as a fiduciary, he has enabled such other fiduciary to commit a breach; or
3. if he has knowledge of a breach by such other fiduciary, unless he makes reasonable efforts under the circumstances to remedy a breach.

A service provider can be considered a fiduciary simply by virtue of rendering investment advice for a fee or other compensation.[13] While some firms will acknowledge their responsibility as a co-fiduciary (which is better than a firm which will not), it does not transfer any liability from the company or its fiduciaries because the plan sponsor still retains full discretion for the plan investments. A co-fiduciary service in many cases has a very limited scope and usually refers to some type of advisory capacity without discretion. You should always ask a service provider who offers any type of co-fiduciary service to clearly explain the extent of these services and get it in writing.

It is beneficial, however, to have a co-fiduciary investment consultant because they are bound by the duties of loyalty, prudence, diversification, and following the plan documents. On the other hand, a company (and its fiduciaries) which prudently selects and appoints an investment manager (or other discretionary fiduciary) can effectively transfer its liability for the responsibilities and duties assumed by the investment manager or other discretionary fiduciary. ERISA provides that named fiduciaries who prudently appoint an investment manager shall not be liable for the acts or omissions of the investment manager as long as they prudently select and monitor the investment manager.[14] Utilizing a "co-fiduciary" service is very different than appointing an investment manager.

As more service providers begin to use the term "co-fiduciary" to gain a marketing advantage, it is important for plan sponsors to clearly understand exactly what this means in terms of the scope of services being provided. If there is no discretion, there is very little, if any, liability protection. A plan sponsor who wishes to accomplish the transfer of responsibility and liability for plan investments should appoint an investment manager or other discretionary fiduciary, not a co-fiduciary service.

As discussed in Chapter 5, selecting and appointing an investment manager is often the best approach for plan fiduciaries and participants. In lieu of this strategy, plan sponsors will want any service provider who provides investment advice to formally acknowledge their co-fiduciary status in writing.

ERISA 404(c) – Fact or Fiction?

As a plan fiduciary, would you be surprised (and frightened) to learn that you have responsibility for the investment decisions that your participants make when they have the ability to self-direct? For an ERISA fiduciary this is the case although common sense would dictate otherwise. Pete Swisher notes "that the converse is true – fiduciaries are responsible for every investment decision, including participant investment decisions – seems counterintuitive and even unfair to many sponsors, yet is the correct baseline."[15]

In terms of participant investment decisions, ERISA 404(c) provides relief for fiduciaries only if certain conditions are met as specified in the Regulation. It permits retirement plan fiduciaries to transfer the responsibility (and liability) for selecting among the available investment options in the plan to participants if two conditions are met:

1. The participant actually directs the investment of their account

2. The plan meets the requirement of the 404(c) regulations

Sounds easy enough, right? Attorney Fred Reish explains "our experience is that very few plans actually comply with 404(c). It is probable that most (perhaps as high as 90%) 401(k) plans do not comply with 404(c), and, as a result, the fiduciaries of those plans are personally responsible for the prudence of the investment decisions made by participants."[16]

This section is not meant to serve as an in-depth discussion of 404(c); however, here are some basic things to know:

- 404(c) is <u>not</u> a "get out of jail free" card for plan fiduciaries

- Compliance with 404(c) is voluntary and must be elected

- If the plan does not comply with all 20 to 25 conditions of 404(c), the fiduciaries may be responsible (i.e. liable) for participant investment decisions
- Many of these conditions center around providing participants with appropriate disclosure and information so they can make informed decisions
- Fiduciaries must still follow a prudent process for selecting and monitoring the investments in the plan and can be held liable if the plan investments are deemed to be imprudent
- Most fiduciaries incorrectly believe their service providers are "taking care of it"

There is much more to know and understand about 404(c) than can be discussed in this book. However, it is safe to say that a plan will fail to obtain relief if a formal 404(c) compliance process is not designed and consistently followed. Designing this process begins with knowing what the requirements are. To help, a 404(c) compliance checklist is provided in Appendix 5.

My last comment on this topic is a personal but important one. I believe that solely focusing on the goal of obtaining 404(c) relief is an inherently non-fiduciary approach because it places the interests of the plan fiduciaries (i.e. protection) ahead of plan participants and beneficiaries. As previously discussed, ERISA 404(a) requires that fiduciaries act solely in the interest of the participants and their beneficiaries for the exclusive purpose of providing benefits. Prudence would suggest that the best way for fiduciaries to satisfy the exclusive purpose requirement is to take greater responsibility for participant retirement success and to design the plan in such a way as to increase the likelihood of achieving this goal. This idea will be discussed in more detail in Chapter 8.

The Critical Role of Documentation and Prudent Process

Documentation is the cornerstone of demonstrating sound fiduciary governance and prudent decision-making. Swisher has noted that "attorneys will tell you that the three keys to winning in court are 'documentation, documentation, documentation.' It's tough to document following a process that is not itself documented."[17]

The first step to sound fiduciary governance is to formally identify all plan fiduciaries and document each person's responsibility to the plan as well as any delegations and/or allocations of fiduciary responsibility to and among all employees, committees, and third parties. In addition, fiduciaries should meet on a regular basis and carefully document these meetings, the topics discussed, and any decisions made. The courts have generally ruled that a decision which is properly and thoroughly considered and discussed should not be found to be a fiduciary breach if it was reasonably determined at the time to be in the best interests of plan participants and beneficiaries. Finally, all documents or paperwork that relate to the plan or the decision-making process should be well organized and kept in an easily accessible, central location. This is most easily accomplished by creating and maintaining a ***"Fiduciary Audit File"*** and a sample can be found in Appendix 4. This tool should serve as the primary source for all plan-related information and should be updated on a regular basis.

Finally, the role of the fiduciary is to focus on procedure, not necessarily outcome – an important distinction. However, that distinction is commonly misunderstood. Focusing on procedure does not mean that outcomes do not matter. Outcomes are the reason for prudent procedures in the first place; otherwise fiduciaries and prudent procedures would be unnecessary. Achieving favorable outcomes, such as securing retirement income, is the reason a retirement plan is subject to fiduciary standards. Thus, favorable outcomes can be expected (though not guaranteed) if procedures are founded upon correct fiduciary principles, and those principles are adhered to in the day-to-day operation of the plan. Fiduciaries who believe that outcomes do not matter are mistaken, revealing an attitude of indifference and lack of care to participants and beneficiaries. Fiduciaries are not expected to predict the future, nor are they required to make the right decision every single time. However, the fiduciary must be able to demonstrate that he/she was prudent and documentation is the critical element in proving this, and do so with the correct attitudes and understanding of the purpose of implementing prudent procedures in the first place. Over time, a sound governance process should lead to the kind of prudent decision-making that drives successful outcomes. This is the essence of ERISA §404(a)(1)(A).

Conclusion

Arbitration and litigation for fiduciary breaches are running at an all-time high, and it is likely that complaints and/or lawsuits alleging plan mismanagement will continue to increase. In cases such as these, the burden of proof for compliance with all provisions of ERISA lies with the plan fiduciaries. It is important to note that liability is not necessarily determined by investment performance, but rather on whether prudent investment practices were followed.[18] The role of the fiduciary is to manage the process, not necessarily to make investment decisions.

Many plan fiduciaries incorrectly assume their service providers have protected them from breaches of fiduciary responsibility or will defend them in the case of legal action. Unfortunately, this is rarely so. While most of the participating companies in the 401(k) industry— record-keepers, brokers, advisors, and fund companies—claim to act in the best interests of investors, this is often not the case. The only protection for a fiduciary is to establish and follow formal and documented procedures that demonstrate prudent process. Fiduciary liability generally arises when a prudent process is either not defined or is inconsistently applied.

Questions To Ask:

1. Based on my role, am I considered a fiduciary to my plan?
2. If so, am I aware that I have personal liability for the decisions I make about the plan?
3. Do I know my fiduciary responsibilities under ERISA?
4. Am I comfortable with being considered a "prudent expert" in overseeing my duties as a fiduciary? If not, have I hired an expert to guide me or to take responsibility for decisions?
5. Have I been prudent in my decision making process? Can I prove this through documentation?
6. Do I understand the prohibited transaction rules and the circumstances that can get me in trouble?
7. Am I aware of any prohibited transactions either I or other plan fiduciaries have engaged in with the plan?
8. Does my plan do the things prescribed in the plan document?
9. Should I consider appointing an "investment manager" or other professional fiduciary and delegating certain fiduciary responsibilities to that person? What must I do to prudently select this person?
10. Has my plan elected to comply with ERISA 404(c)? Have we met the requirements to obtain relief?

CHAPTER 4

Understanding the Players

Part of what makes the retirement plan industry so confusing is the number of different service providers who participate in the process, usually serving in a non-fiduciary capacity. This creates an environment for significant conflicts of interest to exist.

For instance, mutual fund companies share part of their revenue (i.e. ***revenue sharing***) with other service providers to offset or underwrite other plan services such as recordkeeping. Technically, as long as the service provider is not a fiduciary it is allowed to receive compensation in this way. That assertion is currently being tested in the federal courts. Unfortunately, revenue sharing can lead to conflicts which can increase fees, lower investment returns, and makes it difficult to contain plan costs over time. In Chapter 7 I will discuss how revenue sharing and other types of asset-based fees can significantly lower retirement income for participants. When the revenue sharing arrangement is not disclosed, it can create liability for plan fiduciaries because of the duty to know which service providers are being compensated (and how much) and to determine if the compensation is reasonable. In this chapter, I will attempt to clarify the various roles and responsibilities for the different service providers, as well as discuss the general compensation methods of the main players and reveal some of the conflicts of interest that may exist. As you will see, there is a lot of gray area when trying to determine what role(s) each service provider plays, especially when it comes to the acceptance and extent of fiduciary responsibility. My suggestion is to ask a lot of questions of every service provider to your plan to ascertain their duties and responsibilities.

Broker/Registered Representative

What they do: A broker is also known as a "registered representative" and typically works for a brokerage firm, insurance company, or benefits broker. Brokers can be affiliated with a major "wirehouse" firm (e.g., Morgan Stanley, Merrill Lynch, Wachovia, Smith Barney, etc.), a regional firm (e.g., Stifel Nicholas, Edward Jones, etc.), an independent firm (e.g., LPL, Raymond James, Commonwealth, etc.), or an insurance company (e.g., Mass Mutual, Northwestern Mutual, etc.). To make things more confusing, brokers may go by other titles such as Financial Advisor, Financial Consultant, or Account Executive. Brokers are regulated by both the ***Securities and Exchange Commission (SEC)*** and the ***Financial Industry Regulatory Authority (FINRA).*** FINRA was created through the consolidation of the ***National Association of Securities Dealers (or NASD)*** and the member regulation, enforcement, and arbitration functions of the New York Stock Exchange. Brokers may have securities licenses such as the ***Series 7, Series 6,*** and ***Series 63*** and/or ***Series 65.*** A broker's primary job is to serve as the middleman between a client and a product provider. They are non-fiduciary salespeople who have a clear loyalty to their firm and the products/companies they represent. Brokers usually represent one or more providers and are paid by those providers to sell their products to the broker's clients. In addition, most brokers provide services to retirement plan participants such as enrollment and education meetings. Some brokers may also provide services to the plan such as developing an investment policy statement (IPS), plan reporting and analysis, investment consulting and monitoring, and vendor search and selection. Other brokers may work with participants on an individual basis, outside the scope of the services provided to the plan. Finally, brokers generally utilize retail-class retirement plan platforms that carry higher expenses rather than lower-cost, institutional-class retirement plan platforms. The difference between retail and institutional is discussed in Chapter 6.

How they are generally compensated: Brokers must be affiliated with a ***broker-dealer (B/D)*** and can be compensated in a variety of ways, depending on the products they sell or the providers they represent. Brokers are usually compensated by a commission of some sort, otherwise known as ***"indirect"*** compensation. In a mutual fund-based retirement plan, these commissions are usually in the form of ***12b-1 fees*** and generally range from .25 percent to 1.00 percent of the amount invested in each particular mutual fund. These commission rates are usually paid each year to the broker for as long as he or she services the client. In an insurance-based product (such as a ***group annuity***), the commissions are paid to the broker by the insurance company, based on a variety of factors. In insurance-based products, broker compensation may be ***"front-loaded,"*** meaning a higher percentage is paid upfront and a smaller percentage is paid as a ***"trailing commission"*** in subsequent years. For instance, the broker may be paid an upfront commission equal to 1 percent of plan assets and .25 percent of plan assets in subsequent years. When commissions are front-loaded, these products typically have a ***surrender charge*** that locks the company into the product for a specified period of time. This surrender charge usually declines each year until the lock-up period ends and can last anywhere from one year to seven years. For instance, a group annuity may impose a five-year lock-up period with penalties of 5 percent of plan assets in year one, 4 percent in year two, 3 percent in year three, 2 percent in year four and 1 percent in year five. After five years, the company is free to switch the plan to another provider without penalty. The reason for the surrender charge is so the insurance company can ensure that it makes money on the deal, especially if a large amount of compensation is being paid to the broker up front. If the company paid the broker 5 percent at the outset of the relationship and the plan moved after the first year the insurance company would likely lose money. In most cases, the higher the commission to the broker, the higher the total costs of the plan and its participants. One important caveat for plan fiduciaries to understand is that brokers generally do not receive the full commission directly; it is paid to their broker-dealer. For instance, a retirement product provider may pay the broker's B/D a $10,000 commission, but the broker may only receive a 45 percent payout ($4,500). Some brokers will claim they only make $4,500 on the plan which is not accurate because the plan still pays $10,000 in fees to the broker's firm. Understanding fees is covered in more detail Chapter 6.

Conflicts of interest: Unfortunately, brokers usually have significant conflicts of interest that put the participants (and plan fiduciaries) at risk. For instance, since higher commissions generally equate to higher fees, what does the broker recommend to a client if one product pays a 7 percent commission and a similar product pays a 3 percent commission? Alternatively, a broker may be paid higher commissions (such as 12b-1 fees) by certain ***mutual funds*** in a retirement plan. So one mutual fund may pay the broker 1 percent for assets invested in the fund while a comparable mutual fund may only pay the broker .25 percent. In both examples, the broker is incented to recommend the highest commissioned product the client will accept. A broker may also receive a higher commission (or other incentives like free trips) if they steer a certain percentage of business to one provider or another. Since brokers usually do not serve in an acknowledged fiduciary capacity (see below), they are not required to disclose these conflicts of interest. This contrasts with an advisory firm that does serve in an acknowledged fiduciary capacity. A fiduciary has a responsibility to disclose any conflicts of interest that may affect the objectivity of the fiduciary. This is not to say that brokers are unethical. To the contrary, many brokers may be knowledgeable, competent, and caring and strive to do what's best for their clients. Unfortunately, the compensation system makes it difficult for a broker to provide objective advice to their clients.

Do they accept fiduciary responsibility under ERISA: Generally not. Always ask if the broker accepts fiduciary responsibility, to what extent and get it in writing.

Benefits Broker

What they do: Benefits brokers typically provide a variety of products such as group life insurance, health and dental insurance, and disability and long-term care insurance. Many of these companies also sell retirement plan products to employers as an ancillary benefit. Benefits brokers are usually licensed brokers or registered representatives who represent a variety of insurance companies. Thus, the retirement plans they most often sell are insurance-based products such as group annuities.

How they are generally compensated: Benefits brokers usually represent insurance providers and are generally compensated by commissions or other forms of indirect (and often hidden) compensation. Depending on the product, this may include a large commission upfront and a smaller ongoing trailing commission in subsequent years. One thing to be aware of is that group annuity products often include back-end penalties such as surrender charges for terminating the insurance contract before a certain period of time. These charges are to compensate the insurance company because of the large upfront commission paid to the broker.

Conflicts of Interest: The same conflicts of interest exist that are described in the section above with regard to brokers.

Do they accept fiduciary responsibility under ERISA: Generally not. Always ask if the benefits broker accepts fiduciary responsibility, to what extent and get it in writing.

"Pure" (or Fee-Only) Registered Investment Advisor (RIA)

What they do: A "pure" (or fee-only) RIA is an advisory firm that is not dually registered with a broker-dealer and can only accept direct fees rather than commissions. To be dually registered means that a person can act as both an investment adviser representative and a registered representative ("broker/adviser") depending on how services are provided. Some people view being dually registered as the best of both worlds because they can accept both fees and commissions. Unfortunately, this does nothing to eliminate the conflicts of interest that make life as a broker difficult. When I use the term RIA throughout this book, I am referring to a pure RIA. RIAs may provide a broad range of services to the plan, including (but not limited to):

- Plan Design
- Fiduciary Governance Consulting
- Investment Policy Development
- Metrics, Reporting and Analysis

- Investment Consulting, Selection and Monitoring
- Vendor Search & Selection
- Fiduciary Training
- Fee Assessment/Negotiation

As you can see, many of these services *may* also be provided by a broker, although I believe in a much less conflicted way due to the independence of the RIA and its direct compensation structure (see below). However, there is a unique role that an RIA can play that a broker cannot and that is to accept appointments as an ERISA §3(38) "investment manager." It is important to note that not every RIA serves in this capacity. As discussed in Chapter 3, named fiduciaries who prudently select, appoint, and monitor an investment manager can transfer their responsibility (and liability) for plan assets. I make no apologies that I strongly believe this is the best approach for plan participants and fiduciaries.

How they are generally compensated: RIAs receive no indirect compensation such as commissions, finder's fees, 12b-1 fees, revenue-sharing, kickbacks, etc. An RIA is usually compensated solely for providing advisory services and directly by the client. Fees may be based upon a percentage of the assets in the plan (for instance, .25 percent of plan assets regardless of which funds the money is invested in) or a flat-fee (such as $30,000) based on the scope of services provided to the plan. These fees may be paid directly from plan assets (but are always fully disclosed) or directly by the company (outside of plan assets.)

Conflicts of interest: Although no service provider can be completely free of conflicts, I believe RIAs come closest due to their direct methods of compensation (Full disclosure: our firm is a "pure" RIA). An RIA is usually paid strictly for advisory and/or consulting services and is able to be most objective when advising plan fiduciaries. Also, an RIA must disclose any potential conflicts of interest. For this reason, RIAs are usually able to offer the most objective advice to plan fiduciaries and participants. One example of a potential conflict exists when the RIA is compensated by a percentage of plan assets. When a participant retires and has the option to leave his or her money in the plan or to roll it out, the RIA would only benefit if the money stayed in the plan.

Do they accept fiduciary responsibility under ERISA: Yes, but possibly no. This is actually a tricky (and confusing) question, so let me explain. An RIA is subject to the regulations of the Securities and Exchange Commission (SEC) and is governed by the Investment Advisors Act of 1940. Under the 1940 Act, an RIA is legally bound to serve clients in a fiduciary capacity. However, the ERISA definition of fiduciary is found in ERISA §3(21) and involves either discretion or investment advice for a fee. If an RIA is only hired to provide participant education or conduct enrollment meetings (no discretion or advice), he or she would not be considered a fiduciary under the ERISA definition. An RIA that takes discretion or provides investment advice for a fee will be considered an ERISA fiduciary. Therefore, an RIA is always a fiduciary in one sense but may not be considered an ERISA fiduciary based on their relationship to the plan. As previously discussed, the RIA that has been properly appointed as an ERISA-defined "investment manager" and "independent fiduciary" accepts discretion for selecting and monitoring plan investments. In this scenario, the RIA takes on "virtually all of the fiduciary responsibility" for this plan function.[1] An RIA that does not manage plan assets on a discretionary basis, but provides investment advice for a fee is considered a co-fiduciary. Always ask if the RIA accepts fiduciary responsibility, to what extent and get it in writing.

Consultant

What they do: The term "consultant" is one of the more confusing terms in the retirement plan industry because it can be used to describe either a broker or a Registered Investment Advisor (RIA). The best approach is to ask the consultant whether he or she is a broker/registered representative, a pure RIA, or dually registered.

How they are generally compensated: Asset-based fee, commissions, ***flat-fee*** or ***retainer***, depending whether the consultant is a broker or RIA.

Conflicts of interest: It depends on whether the "consultant" is a broker/registered representative or a Registered Investment Advisor. Any indirect or uneven compensation that is earned always creates a conflict of interest.

Do they accept fiduciary responsibility under ERISA: It depends on whether they are a broker or an RIA as well as on the services they provide to the plan. See the sections for each above.

Third-Party Administrator (TPA)

What they do: A TPA serves as a "contract administrator" and may provide consulting services such as plan design and reporting, administration and recordkeeping, contribution processing, statement generation, IRS-required annual filings, and non-discrimination testing. A TPA is not to be confused with the "plan administrator" who is a named fiduciary and the designated person (or entity) responsible for managing the day-to-day operations of the plan. When recordkeeping and administration are provided by separate companies the plan is considered to be "***unbundled.***"

How they are generally compensated: Most TPAs charge a combination of annual fees which may include a flat fee (known as a ***base fee***), a ***per participant fee*** and in some cases an asset-based fee. Many TPAs also receive revenue-sharing (i.e. ***sub-TA fees***) from mutual funds. These fees are discussed in more detail in Chapter 6. Sometimes this revenue is credited back to the plan and used to offset costs while in other cases this revenue is kept and not disclosed to the plan sponsor.

Conflicts of interest: Many TPAs position their services as "free" or "low cost" because they are compensated by fees that are embedded in products or through revenue sharing with other service providers such as mutual funds. When any compensation is earned in an indirect or undisclosed fashion, it creates the opportunity for conflicts to exist.

Do they accept fiduciary responsibility under ERISA: No. A TPA's actions as contract administrator are generally viewed by the Department of Labor as "***ministerial***" and not as fiduciary functions. TPAs could be considered fiduciaries if they provide investment advice for a fee. Although not a clear-cut issue, it could also be argued that a TPA who earns undisclosed revenue sharing payments has set its own compensation and become a fiduciary by doing so.

Record-keeper

What they do: Record-keepers are responsible for keeping track of participant account activity and balances. Services may include processing investment transactions, maintaining a participant and plan sponsor website, handling participant requests for loans or hardship withdrawals, and providing participant and plan sponsor reports, enrollment kits, etc. In some cases, recordkeeping and administration are provided by the same company. This is known as a "***bundled***" plan.

How they are generally compensated: Most record-keepers charge a combination of annual fees which may include a flat fee (known as a base fee), a per participant fee and in some cases an asset-based fee. Many record-keepers also receive revenue sharing (i.e. sub-TA fees) from mutual funds. Sometimes this revenue is credited back to the plan used to offset costs while in other cases this revenue is kept and not disclosed to the plan sponsor.

Conflicts of interest: Many record-keepers position their services as "free" or "low cost" because they are compensated by fees that are embedded in products or through revenue-sharing with other service providers such as mutual funds. When any compensation is earned in an indirect or undisclosed fashion, it creates the opportunity for conflicts to exist.

Do they accept fiduciary responsibility under ERISA: No. A record-keeper's actions are generally viewed by the Department of Labor as "ministerial" and not as fiduciary functions.

Mutual Fund Company

What they do: A mutual fund company or "***fund sponsor***" is, first and foremost, an asset manager or investment company. Their primary job is to manage money for their investors. In the retirement plan industry, this is usually accomplished through open-end mutual funds that are available to plan participants as investment options. Examples of mutual fund companies are Vanguard, Fidelity, PIMCO, and American Funds. Fund companies are registered and regulated by the Securities and Exchange Commission under the ***Investment Company Act of 1940***. Most fund companies also have retirement plan divisions that provide recordkeeping and administration services. In many cases, retirement plan services are an ancillary line of business that serves as a distribution channel to drive additional assets into the fund company's various mutual funds.

How they are generally compensated: Fund companies are primarily compensated through mutual fund fees known as "***expense ratios.***" Expense ratios vary but generally range between .10 and 2.50 percent, depending upon the fund company, the individual mutual funds, and the ***share class***.

Conflicts of interest: Conflicts of interest arise for a mutual fund company when the company also provides retirement plan services. Asset management is much more profitable than fees received for recordkeeping and administration services. Some fund companies require that all investment options within the fund company's retirement plan product (or platform) be ***proprietary*** funds (meaning mutual funds provided by the fund company). More commonly, fund companies have agreements in place with certain other fund companies in order to make ***non-proprietary*** funds available on the 401(k) platform. For instance, T. Rowe Price may allow funds from PIMCO into their 401(k) offering as an available investment option for plan participants. To compensate T. Rowe Price for lost revenue, PIMCO would be required to share a portion of any compensation received from money invested in their funds. This is known as "revenue sharing" and is discussed in Chapter 6. The obvious conflict is that the sponsoring fund company only provides access to fund families who are willing to share revenue, otherwise known as "***pay to play***" arrangements. The sponsoring firm cannot be completely objective if it only considers other fund families that agree to these types of arrangements. In many cases, revenue sharing is not disclosed to plan fiduciaries. If prudence would dictate this revenue sharing to be unreasonable in light of the services provided to the plan, it could cause a potential breach of fiduciary responsibility.

Do they accept fiduciary responsibility under ERISA: Generally not. Always ask if the mutual fund company accepts fiduciary responsibility, to what extent and get it in writing.

Insurance Company

What they do: Insurance companies typically serve as "bundled" providers, meaning they offer a one-stop-shop for retirement plan services. These services could include recordkeeping, administration, investment, and participant education/enrollment. Most insurance company 401(k) plans are actually group variable annuity products which are insurance company contracts. They provide investment options called "***sub-accounts***" that are similar to mutual funds in look and feel. These sub-accounts often carry the same name and are operated by the same companies as publicly offered mutual funds, but they are not the same. Sub-accounts usually have a different and higher expense structure than their mutual fund counterparts, and possibly a far different return. It is often difficult to actually determine all of the specific costs involved in an insurance-based plan because the information is not readily available like publicly offered mutual funds. Usually, the only place to find information about the sub-accounts is on the insurance company's website or in its marketing materials.

How they are generally compensated: In many cases, insurance companies are compensated through ***wrap fees*** embedded in the insurance contract. These fees cover the costs associated with the plan such as recordkeeping, administration, and marketing. The wrap fee is in addition to any investment related fees charged by the sub-accounts. Group annuities also may include ***mortality risk and administrative expenses (M&E Fee)*** which cover the cost of the insurance features of an annuity contract, including the guarantee of a lifetime income payment, interest and expense guarantees, and any death benefit provided during the accumulation period. The insurance company may also receive revenue sharing through alliances with investment management and mutual fund companies. Due to wrap fees, group annuities are generally among the highest cost 401(k) plans and almost always higher than mutual fund-based 401(k) plans.

Conflicts of interest: Insurance companies have many of the same conflicts of interest found in mutual fund companies that offer retirement plan services. Some insurance companies may also be asset managers and provide their own mutual funds. The decision to recommend their own proprietary mutual funds over competitors' funds may create a conflict of interest. Insurance companies also engage in revenue sharing (discussed in Chapter 6) with investment companies and fund managers. Also, many insurance-based 401(k) plans promote minimal start-up and administration fees but then lock clients into the plan for several years by applying a surrender charge penalty for terminating the plan.

Do they accept fiduciary responsibility under ERISA: Generally not. However, some insurance companies have begun to market "co-fiduciary" services for plan fiduciaries. In most cases, these terms make for great marketing copy but do not provide plan sponsors with the protection they think they are receiving. Always ask the insurance company if they accept fiduciary responsibility, to what extent and get it in writing.

Directed Corporate Trustee/Custodian

What they do: A directed trustee/custodian is a financial institution that has the legal responsibility for safekeeping a plan's assets. The custodian may also provide back-office functions such as cash receipt and disbursement functions, trading, and mutual fund settlement services. The custodian will hold title to the assets but usually exercises no oversight of plan administration, investment selection, or performance. The plan sponsor must sign and approve all actions of the directed trustee. All investment instruction is usually received from the plan sponsor, an appointed investment manager, or directly from the plan participants.

How they are generally compensated: Flat annual fees are typically charged for directed trustee services. A percentage of plan assets usually cover trading and custody services.

Conflicts of interest: A custodian is incented to keep assets in the plan if it is compensated through a percentage of plan assets.

Do they accept fiduciary responsibility under ERISA: A directed corporate trustee/custodian serves in a limited co-fiduciary role to safeguard and hold title to plan assets. It has no discretionary authority and must take direction from a named fiduciary. As a co-fiduciary, a directed trustee is not justified in complying with directions that are known to be imprudent or adverse to the interests of the plan participants and beneficiaries.

Discretionary Corporate Trustee

What they do: A fully discretionary trustee takes sole responsibility for all aspects of plan assets. Appointing a discretionary trustee is a fiduciary act, and the plan sponsor must document and be able to demonstrate it was prudent in the selection and appointment of the discretionary trustee. When properly appointed, the fiduciary duties for plan investments will be allocated to the discretionary trustee and will relieve the plan sponsor and its employees of these responsibilities. The plan sponsor will retain only the obligation to prudently select and monitor the performance of the discretionary trustee.

How they are generally compensated: Usually as a percentage of assets in the plan.

Conflicts of interest: When compensated by a percentage of plan assets, the discretionary trustee faces the same potential conflict of interest as an RIA. Namely, the discretionary trustee would only benefit if the money stayed in the plan.

Do they accept fiduciary responsibility under ERISA: Yes. As its name suggests, the discretionary trustee takes sole responsibility and discretion for all aspects of plan assets. As previously stated, discretion is the litmus test for fiduciary responsibility (and thus, liability).

Auditor

What they do: Generally, federal law requires employee benefit plans with 100 or more participants to be audited by an independent, qualified public accountant. The auditor must be licensed or certified as a public accountant by a state regulatory authority. In certain cases, federal law permits the scope of the audit to be limited. Plan fiduciaries should consult their accountant, attorney, or plan advisor to determine whether limiting the scope of an audit is appropriate. When the audit is completed, the auditor will issue a report and state an opinion on the plan's financial statements as well as any schedules required to be included as a part of the plan's annual report filing. Auditors will also report on significant problems, if any were found.

How they are generally compensated: Auditors receive direct fees based on the scope of work provided to the plan. The scope is generally outlined in an ***engagement letter*** which describes the work to be performed, the timing of the audit, and fees. These fees may be charged on an hourly basis or as a flat fee.

Conflicts of interest: If the auditor has financial interests in the plan or plan sponsor, this would affect its ability to render an objective, unbiased opinion about the financial condition of the plan. Also, if the auditor is paid on an hourly basis, it may have a vested interest in billing as many hours as possible for services rendered to the plan.

Do they accept fiduciary responsibility under ERISA: Auditors generally are not fiduciaries when acting solely in their professional capacities. The key to determining whether an individual or an entity is a fiduciary is whether they are exercising discretion or control over the plan.

ERISA Attorney

What they do: ERISA attorneys provide a valuable service to plan fiduciaries. Their advice can limit fiduciary liability and help protect plan participants. ERISA is a very technical and complex area of the law, and a good ERISA attorney can provide an understanding of the practical application of the rules, especially whenever a merger, acquisition, or divestiture takes place.

How they are generally compensated: Fees are usually charged on an hourly basis. In some cases, a flat-fee may be charged based on the scope of work.

Conflicts of interest: If the attorney is paid on an hourly basis, he or she may have a vested interest in billing as many hours as possible for services rendered to the plan.

Do they accept fiduciary responsibility under ERISA: Attorneys generally are not fiduciaries when acting solely in their professional capacities. The key to determining whether an individual or an entity is a fiduciary is whether they are exercising discretion or control over the plan.

Questions To Ask:

1. Do I clearly understand which types of service providers work with my plan and what their roles are?
2. Do I understand how my service providers are compensated?
3. Am I aware of any conflicts of interest that may affect the objectivity of the recommendations/advice I receive from my service providers?
4. Do I know which providers acknowledge fiduciary status and to what extent?

CHAPTER 5

Protecting Participants from Themselves[1]

On February 20, 2008 the Supreme Court ruled unanimously in *LaRue v. DeWolff* that plan participants can sue plan administrators for breaching their fiduciary duties. The good news is that an employer's ability to mitigate most if not all practical day-to-day fiduciary risk is well within their reach. Not only is it economically viable for a plan sponsor to receive protections from fiduciary risk, it is economically viable for participants as well. It is also equally simple. But how?

I believe that high costs, while a major threat to the retirement security of millions of Americans only represents part of the problem. When these costs are combined with less than optimal investment performance, participants are virtually ensured of unsuccessful retirement outcomes.

A study commissioned by John Hancock tracked the performance of 14,487 plan participants from 1997-2006 and compared the results of those participants who selected a professionally managed approach (John Hancock Lifestyle Portfolios) to those who chose to make their own investment decisions (do-it-yourselfers).[2]

The study determined that 84.2 percent of do-it-yourselfers would have fared better in a single professionally managed portfolio than they fared by selecting their own investments. In addition, participants who chose to allocate all their contributions to a single professionally managed approach outperformed do-it-yourself participants by 1.9 percent annually (7.2 vs. 5.3 percent). Do-it-yourselfers as a group ended the period with 11 percent lower account balances.

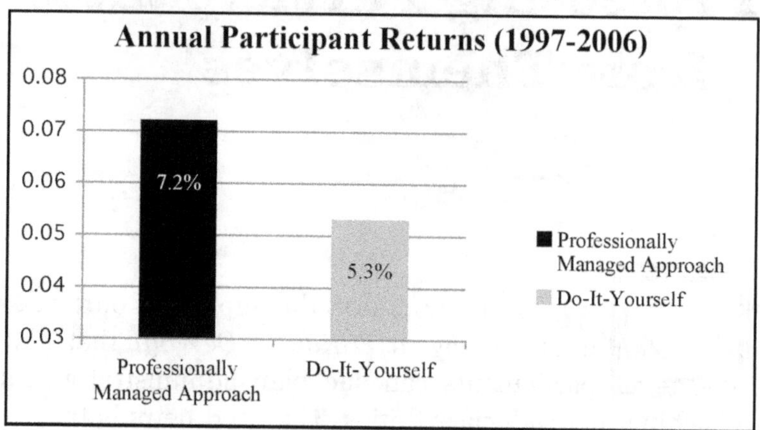

The study also demonstrated that do-it-yourselfers typically shared the following characteristics:

- **Lack of Diversification:** The average number of funds selected was 3.9.
- **Lack of Discipline:** These participants tended to allocate their balances to popular funds at the time of their enrollment and made few changes afterwards (such as systematic rebalancing).
- **An Unbalanced Approach:** These participants tended to allocate their accounts at opposite ends of the risk spectrum (conservative or aggressive) rather than taking a more balanced approach.

Further research paints an even bleaker picture. A recent study by DALBAR Financial Services tracked investor's behavior in chasing market returns from 1987-2006.[3] Over this twenty year period the S&P 500 yielded 11.8 percent per year while the average investor only earned 4.3 percent.

The data clearly demonstrate that the vast majority of participants lack the knowledge, skill, and discipline to make good investment decisions. I believe a better overall approach is for a named fiduciary to appoint an independent investment fiduciary (such as a §3(38) "investment manager") to build and manage model portfolios for participants. The investment manager accepts ERISA "discretion" over plan assets and assumes full responsibility (and therefore liability) for those fiduciary functions.[4] As discussed in Chapter 3, this approach enables the named fiduciary to transfer its liability to the investment manager who takes on virtually all of the fiduciary responsibility.

Noted fiduciaries Jeffrey C. Chang, W. Scott Simon and Gary K. Allen have asserted the value of this approach:

> *Yet few 401(k) plans offer portfolios as investment options. Instead, they offer stand-alone mutual funds or individual stocks as investment options. Such options can be likened to the parts that make up a car. The participants are asked, in effect, to assemble all the parts (i.e., stand-alone investment options) on their own in order to manufacture a car (i.e., a portfolio). With a model portfolio, the parts are already assembled for the participant; all he or she needs to do is provide the ERISA-defined investment manager with enough information so that the manager can select the appropriate car from the menu of five or six investment options that comprise the cars sitting on a showroom floor. There is simply no better way to diversify the risk of a portfolio.*[5]

This professionally managed approach not only benefits the plan sponsor through the transfer of fiduciary responsibility but should deliver better returns over time for plan participants.

Commenting on the *LaRue vs. DeWolff* ruling, attorney George L. Chimento raises a valid question:

> *Are participants really better off self-managing their retirement assets, doing something they were not educated to do? Perhaps it's safer, and better for all parties, just to have an "old fashioned" managed fund, without participant direction, and to employ properly certified investment managers who can be delegated fiduciary liability under ERISA. A dividend of LaRue is that it may cause employers to step back and reconsider the current, expensive, and dangerous fad of self-direction.*[6]

Prudent plan sponsors who understand their duty to act "solely in the interest of the participants and beneficiaries and for the exclusive purpose of providing benefits to participants and their beneficiaries" would be wise to engage an ERISA §3(38) investment manager. This decision alone could determine whether participants "retire with dignity or in despair" as industry expert Brooks Hamilton has stated.[7]

Questions To Ask:

1. What responsibility do I have as a fiduciary to ensure that my participants are having successful investment experiences? Are they?
2. Do we provide professionally managed options (lifestyle funds, target-retirement date funds, balanced funds or managed portfolios) in our plan?
3. Do my participants understand the purpose and value of these options? What percentage uses these options correctly?
4. What must I do to better educate my participants on how to use these options?
5. Should we even provide participants the option to select their own individual funds or should the plan only provide professionally managed "portfolios?"
6. Have we appointed an independent fiduciary such as an ERISA §3(38) investment manager for our plan? If not, could we defend that decision in court? Is our own expertise up to the task?

CHAPTER 6

Deciphering Fees & Expenses

"[A fiduciary] has a specific obligation to ... ensure that fees and expenses are reasonable in light of the level and quality of services provided..."[1]

Matthew D. Hutcheson, a recognized authority on retirement plan economics, has suggested the two primary concerns about the current 401(k) environment are fiduciary indifference and the lack of fee transparency that exists.[2] Sadly, these two issues are closely aligned.

The retirement plan industry has done a poor job of providing clear and easy-to-understand fee disclosure. The majority of plan providers, brokers, investment consultants, brokerage firms, insurance companies, mutual fund companies, and third-party administrators have all contributed to this problem. Unfortunately, the retirement security of millions of plan participants has been put at risk because of hidden fees, high expenses, and conflicts of interest.

However, plan fiduciaries are also guilty for what has transpired because many have failed to take their responsibilities seriously, have not devoted the time necessary to become educated, and have failed to hold their service providers accountable. Many plan fiduciaries have also exposed themselves to significant liability for failing to clearly identify and understand the total cost of their plans. Most importantly, they have failed their participants by allowing costly plans to eat away at retirement savings. One-half of a percent in additional expenses over a 30-year period can reduce retirement income by over 13 percent.[3]

Since a fiduciary has a duty to ensure the plan only pays reasonable expenses, it follows that the fiduciary must know who is being paid and how much compensation is being received for the services provided to the plan. Only by knowing this information can a plan fiduciary decide if the plan fees are reasonable.

The first step to identifying plan fees is to understand the various types that are associated with retirement plans. This by itself is not an easy task. In general, plan fees are paid in four ways:[4]

- ***Asset-Based:*** expenses are based on the amount of assets in the plan and generally are expressed as percentages or ***basis points***.
- ***Per-Person:*** expenses are based upon the number of eligible employees or actual participants in the plan.
- ***Transaction-Based:*** expenses are based on the execution of a particular plan service or transaction.
- ***Flat Rate:*** fixed charge that does not vary, regardless of plan size.

Asset-Based

Asset-based fees are implicit fees that are paid from plan assets and can make it difficult to assess the actual cost in terms of dollars, absent an invoice. These fees are usually expressed as a percentage of plan assets. As Matthew Gnabasik, Managing Director of Blue Prairie Group, points out, asset-based fees now account for nearly 90 percent of the revenue generated by 401(k) service providers.[5] Most service providers love asset-based fees because their revenue grows as plan assets grow. This is an important consideration for plan fiduciaries in order to control and contain costs over time. An abundance of excessive asset-based fees is sure to reduce your participants' retirement income, especially when these fees underwrite services such as recordkeeping, administration, or non-discretionary consulting (see Chapter 7). The following is a list of the different types of asset-based fees that can be assessed to a retirement plan:

- ***Expense Ratios:*** Expense ratios are the fees charged by mutual funds for investment management services. These fees are explicitly disclosed to investors in the fund prospectus or fact sheet and are automatically deducted from participant accounts.
- ***Share Classes:*** Many mutual fund companies have created different share classes for their mutual funds which have different fee schedules associated with them. These different share classes typically provide additional amounts of compensation and revenue sharing to brokers and TPAs. For instance, American Funds has created an R-share class for money invested in retirement plans. The chart below represents the different share classes and expenses for the Growth Fund of America mutual fund:

Share Class	Expense Ratio	Broker's Commission (12b-1)
R-1	1.35%	1.00%
R-2	1.10%	0.75%
R-3	0.85%	0.50%
R-4	0.60%	0.25%
R-5	0.35%	0%

As you can see, the difference between the R-1 and the R-5 share class is 1.00 percent which is solely due to the commission paid to the broker for selling the plan, despite the fact that it's the same basic mutual fund. On a $10 million plan, average plan fees of 1.35 percent equate to $135,000 whereas average fees of .35 percent equate to $35,000. Plan fiduciaries have a responsibility to know what share classes their plan offers and whether the fees being paid are reasonable. Unfortunately, due to lack of disclosure, many fiduciaries have no idea what share classes are offered in their plan or why the decision was made to offer one share class over another (usually to pay the commission to the broker.) Differing share classes create major conflicts of interest for the non-fiduciary broker or advisor. Always ask your service providers which share classes are in the plan, why these were chosen, and if your plan qualifies for a lower cost share class. Better yet, eliminate all indirect compensation from the plan completely.

12b-1 fees: Many mutual funds include 12b-1 fees as part of their operating expense. These fees are used to pay for sales, marketing and distribution costs and usually range from .25 to 1 percent, (otherwise known as 25 to 100 basis points.)[6] This fee usually represents the commission paid to the broker for selling a 401(k) plan. As outlined above, different share classes dictate the amount of 12b-1 fee paid to the broker. 12b-1 fees present two issues for the fiduciary. First, this fee is paid indirectly to the broker and in many cases may not be fully disclosed to plan fiduciaries. Second, some funds may pay higher 12b-1 fees than others which represent a significant conflict of interest. For instance, suppose a plan offers two similar large cap growth funds. Fund A has total expenses of 1.00 and pays the broker a .50 percent 12b-1 fee. Fund B has total fees of 1.50 percent and pays the broker a 1.00 percent 12b-1 fee. The broker has a vested interest to recommend Fund B because he/she stands to make twice the amount of compensation.

Sub-Transfer Agent Fees (or Sub-TA fees): A transfer agent is typically a bank, trust company, or mutual fund that provides services such as shareholder recordkeeping, trade execution, or order settlement.[7] When a transfer agent outsources any of these services to a third-party (such as a TPA), that third-party becomes a sub-transfer agent. Sub-TA fees are paid to the TPA to offset the services rendered to the plan (also known as "revenue sharing"). For instance, a TPA may charge a plan $4,000 for administration but receive another $3,000 in sub-TA fees for total compensation of $7,000. Unfortunately, sub-TA fees are often not disclosed to plan fiduciaries, and the lack of disclosure is what creates the major problem. Sub-TA fees are not inherently wrong, but they are not necessary in a properly designed plan, and they can create fiduciary issues for both the fiduciaries and the TPA if undisclosed. These fees also make it difficult to control plan costs over time (see Chapter 7).

Investment Advisory Fees: Investment advisory fees are usually charged by a Registered Investment Advisor (RIA) who provides investment advice to the plan and/or its participants but takes no discretion (they would serve strictly as investment advisor). In some cases, the RIA may be appointed as an ERISA-defined investment manager and take discretion over some or all plan assets. It is important to note that an RIA does not serve as an investment manager as defined under ERISA unless specifically (and procedurally) appointed. The RIA may construct asset allocation portfolios or managed accounts for participants to invest in. If so, the RIA, working in a discretionary capacity to the plan, would be responsible for managing these portfolios on an ongoing basis for the participants, periodically rebalancing the portfolios, and following a prudent investment process to determine when changes to the underlying investments should take place. This fee is typically charged as a percentage of plan assets and is in addition to the expense ratios charged by the underlying mutual funds. However, if using institutional class pricing (see below) or passive investment strategies, this combination of fees can still be extremely low for the value provided. The RIA should provide the plan sponsor with an invoice (usually quarterly) so the company can authorize the custodian to provide payment. This also ensures the fees are fully disclosed and understood.

Custodian Fees: An asset-based fee that is charged by a custodian for providing back-office functions such as cash receipt and disbursement functions, trading, and mutual fund settlement services. A separate custodian is usually necessary when utilizing an independent record-keeper. Mutual fund and insurance companies typically "bundle" custody services within their 401(k) products. When charged separately, this fee is usually in the .05 percent to .15 percent range.

Wrap Fees: A wrap fee is an all-inclusive annual fee imposed on the value of total assets in a 401(k) plan. Wrap fees are typically charged by insurance providers, who provide a 401(k) plan in the form of a variable group annuity. In these plans, wrap fees typically include mortality and expense fees (M&E fees) and distribution fees in addition to the cost of plan services and investment management (expense ratios).[8] Matthew Hutcheson estimates insurance company charges sometimes range as high as two to four percentage points annually and when added to investment fees can approach 3 percent to 5.5 percent each year.[9]

Mortality Risk and Administrative Expense (M&E Fee): A fee charged by an insurance company to cover the cost of the insurance features of an annuity contract, including the guarantee of a lifetime income payment, interest and expense guarantees, and any death benefit provided during the accumulation period._

Section 28(e) Fees ("Soft Dollars"): Soft dollars are payments that occur between investment companies (i.e., mutual funds) and their service providers, pursuant to SEC rule

28(e). These insidious fees are some of the most difficult to assess because they are embedded into other expenses within a mutual fund and do not show up as actual cash expenses. For instance, if a mutual fund buys research from a brokerage firm with actual cash ("***hard dollars***"), these costs show up in the expense ratio of the fund. However, a mutual fund may be given these products and services by the brokerage firm in exchange for higher than reasonable commissions paid to the firm to execute trades for the fund. If a trade costs five cents per share to execute, the brokerage firm may charge the mutual fund ten cents per share and use the excess commission to offset the cost of the services given to the mutual fund. These soft dollars do not show up in the expense ratio and allows the fund to represent its costs as being lower than they actually are, even though the investor shoulders the burden. Or, as some SEC investigations have shown soft dollars, potentially representing millions of dollars, may be paid to investment consultants by the same mutual funds the consultant has been hired to monitor and supervise. [10] In many cases, these fees are used to buy the consultants' loyalty (i.e., "pay to play") and are inadequately disclosed. Soft dollars are unnecessary fees that provide no benefit to investors.

Trading Costs: Trading costs are some of the most difficult to identify because they either are not (or cannot) be clearly disclosed by mutual fund companies. Investing is not a "frictionless" activity. Each time a mutual fund buys or sells securities within the portfolio it incurs trading costs (such as commissions, bid/ask spreads, market impact, etc.). These costs serve to reduce investor returns. Mutual funds that trade excessively have higher turnover and thus higher trading costs. One way to estimate trading costs is to look in the ***Statement of Additional Information (SAI)*** provided each year by the mutual fund. The SAI will usually list the amount of gross trading commissions paid by the fund. This amount can then be divided by the total assets in the fund for an estimated cost. For instance, if a mutual fund has $100 million in assets and pays $1 million in trading commissions it would incur trading costs of an additional 1.00 percent. As a point of note, actively managed mutual funds generally have higher trading costs than passively managed funds (i.e., index funds) and stock funds have higher trading costs than bond funds.

Per-Person

Administration Fee: Many TPAs will charge a per-participant fee for administration which is often in addition to a flat, base fee (see below).

Investment Advice: Some investment advisors will charge a per-participant fee for providing investment advice to individual participants. In other cases, this fee may be charged as a percentage of assets (asset-based).

Transaction-Based

Start-Up or Conversion Expenses: Many record-keepers and TPAs will charge one-time fees for a start-up plan or to convert a plan from another provider.

Administrative Fees: These fees are typically individually paid by participants for various services and requests. For instance, a small fee may be required by the record-keeper for "events" such as to initiate a loan, to process a distribution, or to mail participant statements.

Sales Loads or Sales Charges: Some providers may assess "front-end loads" or other sales charges when certain share classes of mutual funds are purchased. For instance, a five percent commission may be assessed any time shares of a mutual fund are purchased. This one-time commission or "load" is paid to the broker for the transaction, and ongoing compensation in the form of 12b-1 fees may be received. Expense ratios also still apply. While some small plans may still have this arrangement, most plan providers waive these charges in lieu of asset-based fees such as 12b-1 fees.

Surrender Charges: Insurance companies sometimes include a surrender charge, or early redemption fee, with a group annuity contract if the plan terminates the contract within a specified period of time. Insurance companies include these charges to protect their profitability since they often pay large upfront commissions to the brokers who sell these products. If a large commission is paid at the outset but the plan leaves within a year or two, the insurance company is at risk to lose money. The surrender charge protects the interest of the insurance company by providing compensation in case this happens. Unfortunately, the participants pay the price. The surrender charge is usually determined as a percentage of total assets which goes down over time and eventually goes away. For example, a vendor may charge five percent of the contract if termination occurs in year one, four percent in year two, three percent in year three, and so on, until it expires in year five.

Flat Rate: Flat rate charges are explicit fees that are either billed directly to the plan sponsor or to plan participants.[11] These charges are usually in the form of a flat fee, retainer, or hourly charge and should be clearly stated on the invoice you receive from your service provider. According to Gnabasik, "many service providers have gone out of their way to reduce or even eliminate explicit fees as a way to advertise 'low-cost' or 'no-cost' 401(k) plans... Whenever possible, the plan sponsor should pay for explicit fees since these costs are tax deductible as a business expense. When participants pay, dollars are diverted from tax-advantaged investment growth, which represents a lost opportunity for dividends, interest, and gains."[12] These fees are fully disclosed and may be paid directly by the plan sponsor or from plan assets.

Base Administration Fee: Many TPAs charge a flat, base fee in addition to per participant charges for plan administration.

Consulting Fees: These are billed charges in the form of a flat fee or retainer charged by consulting firms for services such as:

- Fiduciary Governance Consulting
- Investment Policy Development
- Investment Consulting, Selection, and Monitoring
- Participant Education
- Vendor Search and Selection

Audit Fees: Federal law requires that all ERISA-covered plans with more than 100 participants be audited by an independent auditor. It is also common to refer to a DOL or IRS examination of a plan as a plan audit. Any charge imposed by a service provider in connection with this audit is reflected on Schedule B. These fees can be paid directly by the plan sponsor or from plan assets and are generally billed on an hourly basis or as a flat fee.

Attorney Fees: Plans that require the services of an ERISA attorney are generally billed on an hourly basis, as a project fee, or as a retainer.

Which Expenses Can Be Paid By The Plan?

There is often confusion about which types of expenses can be paid by the plan versus the plan sponsor. As a general rule, "operational" expenses may be paid out of the plan while "settlor" expenses must be paid directly by the plan sponsor, and the Department of Labor (DOL) has issued an advisory opinion that clarifies the differences between these expenses.[13] In *401(k) Fiduciary Governance: An Advisor's Guide*, Pete Swisher of Unified Trust states:

> *The dividing line for determining which expenses are chargeable against plan assets is relatively simple: any reasonable expense of operating the plan may be paid by the plan. Any expense associated with a sponsor's business decisions must be paid by the sponsor; these decisions are called "settlor" decisions, since the sponsor is the legal settlor of the trust. Operational expenses may be paid by the plan; settlor expenses must be paid by the sponsor.*[14]

Swisher also gives some clear and helpful examples of these types of expenses:[15]

Examples of settlor expenses include:

- Fees for conducting plan design studies
- Legal fees for amendment of the plan document when the amendment is not required to maintain the plan's qualified status
- Expenses associated with union negotiations on the subject of plan benefits
- Consulting fees to analyze the cost impact of implementing various plan designs
- Plan amendment fees in conjunction with establishing a participant loan program
- That portion of the cost of producing participant enrollment kits that is attributed to information for employees which is not related to the plan

Examples of operational expenses that are clearly permissible expenses of the plan include:

- Investment fees
- Third-party administration expenses
- Expenses associated with maintaining plan qualification status, including non-discrimination testing and mandatory plan amendments
- Trustee fees
- Advisory fees
- Audit fees
- Custodial fees

Plan fiduciaries should pay careful attention to all the fees paid in conjunction with sponsoring the plan and how these fees are paid since errors can lead to prohibited transactions.

A Word on Pricing – Retail vs. Institutional

Mutual funds often have two flavors of the same fund. Retail mutual funds are typically sold by brokers and registered representatives to retail investors and carry higher expense ratios. Institutional versions of mutual funds are typically utilized by select firms such as Registered Investment Advisors (RIAs) and sometimes require high investment minimums (e.g., $1 million). Institutional pricing strips out the costs associated with compensating third parties (via 12b-1 fees or revenue sharing) and can greatly reduce the overall cost to participants. Institutional pricing is most often available in non-bundled plans or independent record-keeping platforms. Many plans, if designed correctly, can utilize institutional share classes although my experience has been that most plans are unaware that they may be eligible for this type of pricing. Ask your service providers if your plan qualifies for institutional share classes.

Conclusion

The impact of excessive fees on long-term retirement savings cannot be understated. The plain and simple truth is costs matter.

The retirement plan industry has operated under a veil of secrecy for far too long. Until service providers are held to a high level of accountability and are required to disclose their fees and compensation, participants will continue to pay the price, both literally and figuratively. Many financial salespeople would have a hard time justifying the cost of the plans they sell if plan fiduciaries actually knew how much compensation was being received in light of the service being provided.

Fee transparency and clear disclosure is good for (almost) everybody involved because it will drive down prices and encourage competition. Participants benefit from lower costs most directly because their account balances will grow more quickly. Plan fiduciaries benefit because they can make better informed decisions and more effectively fulfill their responsibilities. The best service providers will benefit because the true value of their services will become apparent and competition should drive them toward continuous improvement. The only group that does not benefit is the service providers who have made handsome profits for a long time but without providing much value to anyone but themselves.

Interestingly, the industry is most likely going to be forced to change its current practices due to significant pressure from Congress and the Department of Labor. Recently proposed regulations (expected to take effect January 1, 2009) will require service providers, including those who do not serve in a fiduciary capacity, to disclose the amount and types of compensation received as well as any conflicts of interest that exist which may color the objectivity of recommendations made to plan sponsors and participants. Not surprisingly, these proposed regulations have received significant pushback by many members of the retirement plan industry. Stay tuned as this story continues to develop!

Questions To Ask:

1. Am I comfortable with level of proactive fee disclosure provided by my service providers?
2. Do I clearly understand all the fees associated with my plan, both direct and indirect, who is receiving compensation from the plan, and the amount of that compensation in percentages and dollars?
3. How do the fees in my plan compare with other plans that are similar in size and industry?
4. When was the last time I had a detailed fee analysis conducted on my plan by an independent, objective third-party?
5. Do any of the funds in my plan include any revenue sharing in the form of sub-TA fees? How much?
6. Is there any amount of 12b-1 fees included in my plans funds? How much?
7. What share class are the funds in my plan? Why were these share classes chosen?
8. Do we have retail or institutional share classes in the plan? If retail, can we qualify for institutional classes?
9. Do any funds in the plan provide for higher 12b-1 fees than others and create a conflict for the recommendations by our broker, advisor, or consultant?
10. In light of the previous question, should we consider eliminating all funds that provide for any indirect compensation?

CHAPTER 7

Tips for Containing Plan Costs

This chapter will not likely win me many friends and allies in the industry, but it addresses a very important issue – containing plan costs.

I believe the total internal cost for many 401(k) plans is completely out of control. I've already addressed the problem with lack of transparency and the challenge of identifying the many different types of fees that may exist. In this chapter, I would like to offer some tips for plan fiduciaries who desire to fulfill their fiduciary duty to ensure they are being assessed reasonable plan expenses and to provide an effective, low cost 401(k) plan.

The retirement plan industry is big business and generates tremendous fees for companies who sell, advise, and service 401(k) plans. In fact, retirement plans represent more than $16 trillion in assets[1] and are second only to Social Security in impact on national retirement security.[2] In fairness, it costs money to deliver a retirement plan to participants, and multiple service providers need to participate and earn a reasonable profit. Plan sponsors and participants also need their service providers to run profitable businesses. Frankly, our economy needs this too. The question plan sponsors must ask is what represents a reasonable cost for the services rendered to the plan.

The challenge to "***cost containment***" is that the retirement plan industry is addicted to charging asset-based fees for services that should not be billed this way. Do not get me wrong: there are certain services that need and should be billed this way. However, too many layers of asset-based fees are the enemy to your participant's retirement success and your plan's total costs.

Service providers love these types of fee arrangements because they virtually guarantee a growing stream of income as long as the plan sponsor remains a client.

Unfortunately, plan participants will realize reduced streams of income during their retirement because they were denied the benefits of economies of scale that they rightfully deserved during their years of saving for retirement.

In my opinion, the two areas where asset-based fees do not make sense are for record-keeping and administration services, and for ongoing commissions (such as 12b-1 fees) for brokers/advisors/consultants who do not manage plan assets on a discretionary basis. Let me explain.

Many record-keeping firms and TPAs receive asset-based fees for their services which may or may not be disclosed (i.e., revenue sharing). For instance, a record-keeper may charge a company a flat base fee, a per-participant fee, and a fee based on a percentage of plan assets. The chart below shows a simple example of two plans – one with 100 participants and $3,000,000 in assets and the other with 100 participants and $6,000,000 in assets.

Fees	Plan A	Plan B
Base fee	$3,000	$3,000
Per participant fee ($20)	$2,000	$2,000
Asset-based fees (.15%)	$4,500	$9,000
Total fees	$9,500	$14,000
Total fees (per participant)	$95	$140

Although each plan has the same number of participants (and presumably requires the same basic amount of work), the record-keeper receives an additional $4,500 in compensation for Plan B simply because the assets are greater. This represents a 47 percent difference for the same basic services rendered to each plan. As the plan assets continue to grow, the record-keeper's compensation will increase at the expense of participant account balances, resulting in less retirement income. Frankly, this is one way expenses spiral out of control. Recordkeeping services <u>should not</u> be subsidized by asset-based fees, but rather, by flat rate and per-participant fees tied to the scope of services provided to the plan.

In the example above, the record-keeper should charge the amount that is required to deliver its services profitably to 100 participants. If the plan still has 100 participants during the next year, the administration fees should increase by some reasonable amount due to increases in the cost of doing business, but there should not be a difference of 47 percent for services that are unrelated to the total amount of plan assets.

One argument I hear from record-keepers when I present this scenario is how they run the risk of reduced profitability if the plan grows in number of participants, and thus, administrative work. Asset-based fees guarantee their compensation keeps up with their workload. This is a weak argument that demonstrates the industry's addiction to asset-based revenue.

My response is to price services that include both the cost of delivery plus a reasonable profit margin that reflects the level of effort, value, and risk associated with providing services to the plan. Regardless of whether a record-keeper needs $95 or $140 per participant to deliver services profitably, the fee will increase with any additional participants (and the corresponding workload). For instance, if the per-participant fee is $95 and the number of plan participants grows to 150 during the next year, the record-keeper will receive $14,250 ($95 x 150 participants) in compensation for services rendered to the plan.

Too many plan sponsors fail to grasp this concept, often because they have no idea their record-keeper and/or TPA is receiving asset-based fees. As previously discussed, plan fiduciaries have a responsibility to know what the plan is paying in fees and to determine if these fees are reasonable.

Tip #1

Require record-keepers and TPAs to bill their services as a total flat dollar amount (explicitly billed costs). Any asset-based or implicit fees (revenue sharing or sub-TA fees) earned by the service provider should be credited back to the plan to offset explicitly billed costs. If your service provider refuses, take your business elsewhere.

The second area where plan fees can spiral out of control is when it comes to broker/advisor/consultant compensation, via either a 12b-1 fee or an asset-based fee. Many brokers/advisors/consultants (referred to collectively as "investment consultants" for the rest of this chapter) claim they "manage" retirement plans. In most cases, the term "manage" is actually a misnomer. There are two cases where money associated with a retirement plan is actually "managed" and I believe asset-based fees are appropriate:

Plan Investments: Mutual funds, Exchange-Trade Funds (ETFs), separate accounts, or collective trusts.

Discretionary Management: In some cases, a plan may hire a Registered Investment Advisor (RIA) to serve as an ERISA §3(38) investment manager. The RIA manages plan assets on a discretionary basis for the participants (such as building and maintaining model portfolios using the underlying plan investments in a participant-directed plan) or for the plan itself (as in a trustee-directed plan). In either case, the RIA has a direct impact on how the plan assets perform and assumes sole fiduciary responsibility for these functions by taking "discretion."

An investment consultant does not "manage" retirement plans without actually taking discretion. Instead, the investment consultant may "advise" or "consult" to the plan and its participants in a variety of different ways.

"Advising" may mean selling the plan sponsor on which 401(k) provider to choose, helping pick the mutual funds in the plan (watch out for conflicts of interest), and then educating and enrolling participants in the plan. In some cases it may also include "consulting" services such as helping the plan fiduciaries develop an ***Investment Policy Statement (IPS)*** and even providing recommendations on investment selection and ongoing monitoring. While these are all important and necessary steps, the investment consultant does not have direct decision-making authority (discretion) on how the money is actually invested and managed.

This is similar to the scenario with record-keepers and TPAs. The investment consultant provides valuable services to plan and should receive fair and reasonable compensation for those services. However, I believe a fairer method of compensation for non-discretionary services is to charge a flat fee based on the scope of work provided to the plan.

The chart below shows our example of the plan with 100 participants and $3,000,000 in and the plan with 100 participants and $6,000,000 in assets:

Fees	Plan A	Plan B
Asset-based fees (.50%)	$15,000	$30,000
Total fees (per participant)	$150	$300

The investment consultant's pay doubled even though the services have no direct impact on the growth of plan assets. Unfortunately, investment consultants who serve in a non-discretionary (and/or non-fiduciary) capacity often view asset-based fees as an inalienable right since it guarantees them a growing stream of income even if they are not playing a direct role in the growth of plan assets. Interestingly, asset-based fees are much better for your service providers than for your participants who are virtually ensured of a reduced stream of income in retirement. Smart plan fiduciaries recognize this fact, and, unless they appoint an "investment manager" or other discretionary fiduciary, they negotiate flat fees with their investment consultant and require them to acknowledge their role as a "co-fiduciary." Each year, an increase in the fee should be considered depending upon factors such as time, expertise, the value provided, and risk assumed.

Tip #2

Require investment consultants who do not serve as an "investment manager" to assume co-fiduciary responsibility and bill their services as a total flat dollar amount (explicitly billed costs). Any asset-based or implicit fees (12b-1 fees) earned by the service provider should be credited back to the plan and offset explicitly billed costs. If your investment consultant refuses to receive compensation in this capacity, take your business elsewhere.

Finally, plan fiduciaries should negotiate for lower fees and ***fee caps*** with their service providers as plan assets grow. More assets mean more leverage. A $2 billion plan should have much lower relative expenses (as a percentage of assets) than a $2 million plan. Smart plan fiduciaries identify all the costs associated with their plan and use this information to negotiate with their vendors. Winning a new plan is a long and arduous process for every service provider and competition is intense – use this to your advantage. Plus, plan fiduciaries actually have a legal responsibility to negotiate lower fees for their participants. Hiring an independent fiduciary is a good step in this process, since pricing leverage only comes where fee transparency exists and competition is encouraged. Unfortunately, non-fiduciary service providers have no incentive to encourage such activity. An independent fiduciary should be knowledgeable about plan fees and be able to hold service providers accountable and even negotiate lower fees in many instances.

Tip #3

Hire an independent fiduciary to identify ALL plan costs and negotiate with service providers for lower fees. Shop the plan to other vendors to promote competition and require full fee transparency for all services provided to the plan. Make sure to have each vendor attest to this information in writing and have its compliance department sign off on it.

Cost Containment

Containing plan costs is the responsibility of every plan fiduciary. Each company that provides necessary services to the plan should receive fair and reasonable compensation for its work. However, asset-based fees should be held to a minimum so as to contain costs over time. I believe asset-based fees should only be paid to mutual funds and RIAs who serve as ERISA-defined "investment managers" and manage plan assets on a discretionary basis. Plan fiduciaries should always remember that costs matter and make a major impact on your participants' retirement income and security. Higher fees almost always lead to lower benefits.

Questions To Ask:

1. How is each service provided to my plan paid for?
2. Are recordkeeping and administration services strictly paid for with direct fees or are any portion underwritten by an asset-based fees (sub-TA fees)?
3. If sub-TA fees are included in my plan's funds, are they credited back to the plan to offset the direct fees?
4. What steps can I take to reduce or eliminate certain asset-based fees in my plan? Which ones?
5. Does my investment consultant receive asset-based fees or direct fees for services rendered to the plan? Is any discretion being taken?
6. How much compensation in terms of percentages <u>and</u> dollars are my service providers receiving?
7. Is this compensation reasonable in light of the services they provide?
8. Do my service providers deserve a significant "raise" when the plan's assets increase if the services they provide have no bearing on the increase?
9. Can I receive the same or additional services for the plan at a comparable or lower cost?
10. Should I negotiate to only pay direct fees with my service providers unless discretion is being taken?
11. Should I hire an independent fiduciary to conduct a detailed fee analysis and recommend strategies for reducing and containing plan costs?

Chapter 8

PPA and Successful Plan Design

With the passage of the Pension Protection Act of 2006 (PPA), Congress has set forth specific guidelines for what it believes constitutes a successfully designed retirement plan. This chapter highlights some of the key provisions set forth in the legislation which should be considered by plan fiduciaries. Several of the new provisions are aimed at improving three areas:

1. Increased participation
2. Greater contribution levels
3. Better investment decisions

Automatic Enrollment

According to the Department of Labor, approximately one-third of eligible workers do not participate in their employers' defined-contribution plan. Behavioral research studies have shown that automatically enrolling employees (in which workers "***opt-out***" of plan participation rather than "***opt-in***") could reduce this rate to less than 10 percent, significantly increasing retirement savings.[1]

The PPA allows employers to automatically enroll employees and increase their contributions without their explicit approval as long as employees are notified. The PPA also provides ERISA preemption to state laws that often prohibit employers from taking paycheck deductions without the employee's written permission, as long as the conditions discussed below are met. The state preemption was previously a barrier to implementing automatic enrollment because many employers were fearful that an automatic enrollment feature could violate certain state payroll-withholding laws and thus subject the employer to lawsuits by plan participants.

On November 7, 2007 the IRS released proposed 401(k) automatic enrollment regulations. Generally, the new rules are effective beginning January 1, 2008. To encourage the adoption of automatic contribution arrangements (ACAs), the proposal covers two additional types under the PPA: Qualified Automatic Contribution Arrangements (QACA) and Eligible Automatic Contribution Arrangements (EACA).

For plan years beginning on or after January 1, 2008, the nondiscrimination testing requirements as well as the top-heavy rules are waived for plans that qualify as a QACA. These arrangements are often referred to as automatic enrollment safe harbor plans as opposed to a "regular" 401(k) safe harbor plan. As with other 401(k) plan safe harbors, amendments adopting the QACA safe harbor must be adopted before the first day of the plan year and remain in effect for the entire plan year. Plan sponsors must furnish a notice to participants at least 30 days (and no more than 90 days) before the beginning of each plan year. The notice must explain the QACA and inform participants of the opportunity to elect out of the program or to change their deferral percentages from the QACA's qualified percentages.

To qualify for the QACA, the plan must meet the following requirements:

- The initial automatic enrollment amount must be at least 3 percent (but not more than 10 percent) of pay and the deferral amount must be increased each year (see annual increase chart below)

- Provide for either matching contributions or non-elective contributions on behalf of non-highly compensated employees as follows:
    - Matching contributions - 100 percent of elective contributions up to 1 percent of compensation and 50 percent of elective contributions between 1 percent and 6 percent of compensation
    - Non-elective contributions - 3 percent of every eligible employee's compensation, regardless of whether the employee participates in the plan

If you currently have a 401(k) safe harbor plan, you may notice the minimum rate of matching contributions for a QACA is less than that for your current plan. Also, employer contributions under a QACA have a two-year vesting period as opposed to immediate vesting as required by other 401(k) safe harbors. This should be an attractive feature for employers desiring to retain employees.

The PPA also added a provision permitting (but not requiring) a plan to allow any employee who has default contributions made under an EACA to withdraw those contributions (with gains/losses). Generally, the election must be made no later than 90 days after the date of the first default elective contribution under the EACA. The withdrawal amount is considered taxable income to the employee in the year withdrawn but is not subject to the 10 percent early withdrawal penalty. Also, any matching contributions must be forfeited. EACA withdrawal privileges do not have to be provided to all affected employees, and the 401(k) plan does not have to be a QACA to take advantage of the EACA rules. Each eligible employee under an EACA must also be given a written notice (subject to the general regulations concerning the use of electronic media) of his or her rights and obligations under the arrangement, within a "reasonable period" before each plan year. The proposed regulations also permits the plan to distribute excess contributions and excess aggregate contributions to participants to correct failed ADP and ACP tests within six months (rather than 2½ months) after the close of the plan year in which the contributions were made. This gives plans more time to make corrective distributions without the employer having to pay a 10 percent excise tax.

Generally, the timing of the QACA, EACA and QDIA notices (see below) are coordinated, so that one notice can be used to satisfy notice requirements under each set of rules.

To have fiduciary protection surrounding investment of automatic contributions in an EACA, employers must invest the automatic enrollment contributions in a "qualified default investment alternative" (QDIA). With a QDIA, the participant can be automatically enrolled and have his/her money automatically invested in the appropriate QDIA, and the plan sponsor is protected from liability. Also, participants and beneficiaries must have the opportunity to direct investments out of a QDIA as frequently as from other plan investments, but at least quarterly. Curiously, a QACA is not required to utilize a QDIA for automatic contributions, although the plan sponsor will likely wish to utilize one to receive liability protection.

Key Elements to Automatic Enrollment

- Provide employees with at least 30 days advance notice (and no more than 90 days) before the plan year. The notice must explain the QACA and inform participants of the opportunity to elect out of the program or to change their deferral percentages from the QACA's qualified percentages.
- Each eligible employee under an EACA must be given a written notice (subject to the general regulations concerning the use of electronic media) of his

or her rights and obligations under the arrangement, within a "reasonable period" before each plan year.

- If implementing a QACA, the plan must incorporate automatic deferral increases (see section below).
- A QACA provides for a two-year vest on employer contributions.
- With an EACA, an employee can opt out of automatic contributions after they have begun and can withdraw contributions made under an automatic contribution arrangement provided the withdrawal occurs within 90 days after the first automatic employee contribution is made. There is no 10 percent early distribution penalty tax on these withdrawals.
- For an EACA, automatic contributions must be invested in a QDIA – this is optional for a QACA.
- Participants and beneficiaries must have the opportunity to direct investments out of a QDIA as frequently as from other plan investments, but at least quarterly.
- A notice must be furnished to participants and beneficiaries in advance of the first investment in the QDIA and annually thereafter.
- Generally, the timing of the QACA, EACA, and QDIA notices may be coordinated, so that one notice can be used to satisfy notice requirements under each set of rules.

Automatic Deferral Increases

The most important factor of retirement accumulation is the level of contribution to the plan. As mentioned above, automatic deferral increases are only <u>required</u> for a QACA. Plan sponsors start employees at a deferral rate (usually 3 or

4 percent) and then increase the deferral rates by a certain percentage each year (usually 1 to 3 percent). Just like the automatic enrollment provision, employees can "opt-out" of the automatic increases at any time. If they do not file an election to opt-out their deferrals will be automatically increased each year to a maximum of 10 percent.

By implementing an automatic deferral increase provision, employers can help their employees contribute higher amounts to retirement savings which increases the probability that participants will retire with sufficient benefits.

Plans that implement automatic deferral increases through a QACA are required to increase the deferrals according to the schedule listed below.

Annual Increase Requirements	
Timeframe	**Required Deferral Percentage**
Initial (Default) Contribution	3% to 10%
Year 2	At least 4%
Year 3	At least 5%
Year 4 and beyond	At least 6%

Qualified Default Investment Alternative (QDIA)

The "qualified default investment alternative" (QDIA) is the cornerstone of improving participant investment experiences and protecting plan fiduciaries. As discussed in Chapter 5, most participants are ill-equipped to make good investment decisions for themselves. The intent of the QDIA is to provide a single investment strategy capable of meeting participants' long-term retirement savings needs as opposed to defaulting them into a low-risk, low-return vehicle such as a money market account or stable-value fund.

The PPA provides for four types of QDIAs:[2]

1. A product with a mix of investments that takes into account the individual's age or retirement date (an

example of such a product could be a ***lifecycle*** or ***target retirement-date fund***)

2. An investment service that allocates contributions among existing plan options to provide an asset mix that takes into account the individual's age or retirement date (an example of such a service could be a ***professionally managed account***)

3. A product with a mix of investments that takes into account the characteristics of the group of employees as a whole, rather than each individual (an example of such a product could be a ***balanced fund***)

4. A ***capital preservation product*** for only the first 120 days of participation (an option for plan sponsors wishing to simplify administration if workers opt-out of participation before incurring an additional tax)

It is important to understand that there are significant differences between each QDIA, most noticeably between a managed account approach and a lifecycle or target-retirement date fund. A prudent plan sponsor should consider the benefits and challenges of each type (as well as potential conflicts of interest) before selecting an approach.

Conclusion

The Pension Protection Act of 2006 is sweeping legislation that provides important and beneficial plan design options for plan fiduciaries to consider. I believe Congress has spoken on how it believes an outcome-focused retirement plan should be designed. Although the information above only provides a brief overview about a few features of the PPA, I hope it spurs you to consider how to incorporate these (and other) new elements into your own plan design.

Questions To Ask:

1. Is my plan currently designed for the success of my participants?
2. Have I implemented any of the plan design provisions encouraged by the Pension Protection Act? If not, why not?
3. If we have not done so yet, should we reconsider?
4. Do I fully understand the structural differences in how the various Qualified Default Investment Alternatives (QDIAs) are designed and implemented?
5. Do I know the benefits and drawbacks to each QDIA?
6. Which one is right for my plan?

CHAPTER 9

Developing an Investment Policy

As outlined in Chapter 5, achieving a successful investment experience should be the goal of every retirement plan participant. Focusing on this goal allows employees to accumulate meaningful retirement assets and helps minimize or even eliminate the stress they feel about the investment process, allowing them to stay focused on the long-term rather than worrying about short-term performance.

Generally speaking, I believe this goal is best achieved when a plan fiduciary prudently selects and appoints an ERISA §3(38) "investment manager" to oversee plan assets on a discretionary basis (see Chapter 5). However, in some cases, the named fiduciaries of an ERISA plan will retain the responsibility (and liability) for making investment decisions. In this situation, the goal for the plan fiduciaries should be to put participants in the best position to achieve a successful experience. This is accomplished by making prudent decisions from a plan design and investment selection standpoint. By doing so, the plan fiduciaries can help their participants fully benefit from the wealth creation that comes from long-term market appreciation.

Capital markets have been shown to work effectively over time and to deliver attractive rates of return. A successful investment experience is one that enables the participant to achieve market rates of return. This approach stands in contrast to strategies that try to outperform the market. Significant amounts of research show this "active" style of investing to be extremely difficult to do successfully over time.

The role of the plan fiduciaries is to help participants focus on the elements they can control rather than those they cannot. There are four aspects of the investment process that are within a retirement plan participant's control:

- Being disciplined
- Being globally diversified
- Controlling costs
- Minimizing taxes

Unfortunately, most participants tend to focus on things that are not within their control (such as stock market performance, direction of interest rates, currencies, etc.) which leads to an unsuccessful investment experience.

Most plan fiduciaries fail to help their participants focus on the things they can control because they do not develop a sound investment policy for the plan. The first step in creating an effective investment policy is to identify which asset classes should be included in the plan. Studies have shown that long-term performance comes primarily from ***portfolio*** structure (i.e., which asset classes to utilize) as opposed to security (or fund) selection and ***market timing***.[1]

Capital markets are composed of many classes of securities, including stocks and bonds, both domestic and international. A group of securities with shared economic traits is commonly referred to as an asset class. There are several asset classes, all with risk and return characteristics that are distinct from one another. Your participants can benefit by combining these different asset classes in a structured portfolio.

A full range of asset classes may include small and large

stocks, domestic and international stocks, value and growth, emerging market countries, global bonds, real estate, and even commodities.

Because asset classes play different roles within a portfolio, the whole is often greater than the sum of its parts. Participants have the ability to achieve greater expected returns with less price fluctuation and more consistency than they would in a less comprehensive (or less diversified) approach.

Structuring an investment strategy around specific asset classes lends purpose to the investment selection process at the plan level as well as at the individual participant level. Rather than analyzing individual securities or mutual funds, investing becomes a relatively simple matter of deciding how much stock to hold versus bonds, and how small or large, and value- or growth-tilted the stocks should be.

Plan fiduciaries tend to fall short during the investment policy development phase because they allow non-fiduciary service providers with significant conflicts of interest to dictate the process for them, rather than utilize an objective third-party to help them structure and drive a formal evaluation process. Many fiduciaries rely on their non-fiduciary investment consultant or 401(k) provider (in many cases a mutual fund company) to recommend a proposed mutual fund lineup during the sales process. Unfortunately, this presents two significant challenges for the plan fiduciaries to overcome.

First, these service providers usually do not serve in a fiduciary capacity to the plan and have undisclosed conflicts of interest that color the objectivity of their recommendations. As discussed in Chapter 6, lack of fee transparency and disclosure with regard to indirect compensation and revenue sharing makes it very difficult for the plan fiduciaries to determine the motivations of the investment consultant or 401(k) provider making the recommendations. This may represent a breach of fiduciary duty for the plan fiduciary. If a non-fiduciary investment consultant is indirectly compensated by commissions for selling the plan, he or she may recommend funds that pay higher levels of compensation (usually with higher expenses) as opposed to lower cost (and lower commission) funds that may be better for the participants. Also, many 401(k) providers are actually mutual fund companies first and foremost and have a vested interest in seeing as much money as possible flow into their family of funds rather than competing fund families. As non-fiduciaries, these service providers are obligated neither to disclose these facts nor to recommend what is best for the plan (the proverbial "fox in the hen house"). Unfortunately, this may negatively impact participants and put plan fiduciaries at risk if it impedes their ability to make prudent and objective decisions.

Second, without a consistent investment selection process, it is nearly impossible for the plan fiduciaries to make a clear comparison of fund recommendations from different providers. For instance, suppose a plan fiduciary was mainly focused on fund performance for the previous twelve months (a mistaken, but not uncommon scenario) and asked two mutual fund companies to put forth their recommended mutual fund lineups. Let us also assume that international stocks performed exceptionally well over this period – much better, in fact, than U.S. stocks. Finally, assume that fund company A proposed an equity lineup consisting entirely of U.S. stock funds while fund company B proposed a lineup that included several international stock funds.

It is likely that fund company B would appear much more attractive because the performance of their recommended funds included an asset class (international stocks) that had great recent performance. Does that mean that fund company B's recommendations are going to perform better over the next twelve months, two years, or ten years? Not necessarily. In fact, prudent plan fiduciaries recognize that past performance serves, at best, as an unreliable predictor of future performance. A more reliable approach is to evaluate investment options by their asset class, fees, how closely the fund tracks a specified ***benchmark index*** over time, and how much turnover takes place within the fund.

Formalizing the Investment Policy

In the example above, the plan fiduciaries are skipping the first step in the investment selection process and putting the cart before the horse. To provide a more accurate comparison, the fiduciaries should first identify the asset classes that will be available in the plan and then require both fund providers to present their fund recommendations for each specific asset class. Next, the plan fiduciary should consider important factors such as share class, expense ratio, style drift, turnover, and performance of the funds proposed for each asset class to make his or her selection. Doing so provides for a more meaningful comparison between the proposed options.

A good "best practice" is to formalize the investment policy development process by creating an Investment Policy Statement (IPS) which puts the investment strategy in writing and commits the fiduciaries to a disciplined approach. All investment decisions for the plan should be determined according to the clearly stated guidelines in the IPS and it should be reviewed each quarter and updated as necessary.

Although an IPS is not required, ERISA states that plans must have some type of documented process for making investment decisions.[2]

Benefits of an Objective Perspective

We have found that most plan fiduciaries and their service providers are poorly equipped to lead a prudent investment selection process, either because of insufficient knowledge or conflicts of interest. Often, the best solution is to hire an independent Registered Investment Advisor (RIA) who serves in a fiduciary capacity and is compensated in the form of fees that are paid directly by the company or from plan assets, rather than commissions from mutual funds or plan providers. Taking this approach ensures the plan fiduciary will receive truly objective advice, make prudent investment decisions that will benefit their participants, and ensure that a sound fiduciary investment process has been implemented and followed.

Questions To Ask:

1. Does my plan have a formal investment policy?
2. Has it been codified in writing with an Investment Policy Statement (IPS)?
3. Who developed it? If a service provider developed it, are there any conflicts of interest that could affect which specific investments he or she recommends?
4. Do we follow the process specified in our IPS?
5. When was the last time we reviewed and updated the IPS?
6. Which asset classes are included in our plan?
7. Why were these asset classes selected?
8. Are there any asset classes or funds that should be added or eliminated from the plan?
9. Do we regularly monitor the plan investments against their comparable benchmark indexes? Can we prove it with documentation?
10. What is our process for removing an asset class or fund?
11. When was the last time we did it?

CHAPTER 10

Choosing Active vs. Passive Investments

Once you have created the investment policy for the plan, decisions need to be made about what specific investment options will be available (e.g., mutual funds). Within the financial services industry a great debate rages over ***active management*** vs. ***passive management*** – two different investing styles. Active management is the art of stock picking and market timing. Active managers focus on identifying securities that are either "undervalued" or "overvalued" and try to outperform or beat the market (often defined as the S&P 500). Bill Miller, the manager of Legg Mason Value Trust, is an example of an active manager and many people are familiar with his track record of beating the S&P 500 Index for fifteen straight years.

Passive management is most often characterized by index funds and Exchange-Traded Funds (ETFs). Passive managers attempt to replicate broad market indexes by purchasing the securities that compose them. The goal is to attempt to match market index returns rather than achieve better-than-market returns. For instance, if the S&P 500 Index returns 10 percent in a given year, an S&P 500 Index Fund will attempt to match this return as closely as possible, minus expenses. John Bogle, the founder of Vanguard Investments, is arguably the most well-known proponent of passive investing. Bogle created and introduced the first index fund, Vanguard 500, in 1976. The argument for passive management is based upon the efficient market theory which suggests that market prices reflect the knowledge and expectations of all investors. This theory asserts that any new development is instantaneously priced into a security, thus making it impossible to consistently beat the market.

The chart below provides a basic comparison of these two styles of investing:

	Active	Passive
Goal	Beat the market index	Match the market index
Success Rate	Hard to achieve consistently	Easy to achieve consistently
Costs	Usually higher	Usually lower
Premise	Securities are "overvalued" or "undervalued"	Securities are fairly priced
Turnover	Usually higher	Usually lower

So which investment style is best? Academic studies and real world experience show that active managers have a hard time consistently outperforming market indexes, in large part because of the high expenses (some which are disclosed to the investor and some which are not) associated with active management.

For instance, ***turnover*** occurs whenever a mutual fund buys or sells the underlying securities within the fund. For instance, a fund with 100 percent turnover buys and sells the entire portfolio in a given year while a fund with 200 percent turnover buys and sells the entire portfolio twice in a given year. Each time a trade takes place, the fund incurs transaction fees known as "trading costs," and these fees serve to reduce the investors' return and, ultimately, retirement income. Unfortunately, trading costs are not disclosed to investors as part of the expense ratio and can be difficult to identify and quantify.

On average, a fund with 100 percent annual turnover loses nearly 1 percent in trading costs.[1] William Harding, an analyst with Morningstar, says the average turnover ratio for an actively managed domestic stock fund is 130 percent.[2] If a mutual fund manager turns over the portfolio 130 percent each year, investors are paying roughly 1.3 percent in trading costs in addition to the fund's expense ratio.[3] Things are not always what they seem in the financial services industry.

Actively managed funds generally have higher turnover which leads to higher trading costs (often dramatically), making it even more likely that this type of fund will fall short of its benchmark. In contrast, passively managed funds typically have much lower explicit costs (i.e., expense ratios) as well as implicit costs (i.e., trading costs) due to lower turnover.

The study referenced below shows that only 2.5 percent of 355 mutual funds outperformed the S&P 500 Index during the period from 1970-2000.[4]

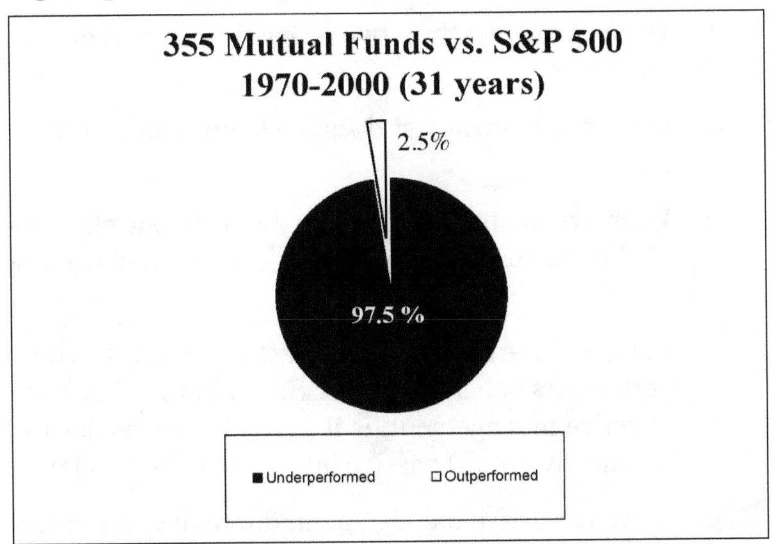

Studies such as this illustrate the difficulty for active managers to outperform their benchmark index any given year, and, over longer periods of time, the case for passive management becomes even more compelling. This is mainly because no reliable way exists to determine which active managers will be among the small number who will outperform in future years (i.e., past performance has little to no correlation to future results). This does not necessarily mean that no one can pick winning stocks; just that it is a very rare skill that is almost impossible to identify in advance and even more difficult to maintain for the long term.

Your participants will probably do far better over time (and at a much lower cost) by investing in a diversified portfolio of index funds rather than trying to select which actively managed funds will prevail each year. I would recommend that a healthy dose (or more) of your plan's investments be based on passively managed strategies.

Questions To Ask:

1. Do we have mostly active or passive investments in our plan?
2. How much turnover does each fund in our plan have?
3. What are the total costs of the funds in our plan, including the expense ratio plus the estimated trading costs?
4. In light of the difficulty for an active manager to outperform its benchmark over time and the high costs of active management, is it prudent to consider using mostly (or all) passive investments in the plan?
5. If we use active management, do we have a process for prudent selection and oversight that we can document as having a reasonable, statistically valid expectation of success?

Chapter 11

The Ideal 401(k) Plan

Although I believe the ideal 401(k) plan is a rarity today, it is well within the reach of just about every organization. To review, the purpose of any 401(k) plan is to deliver successful outcomes and meaningful retirement benefits for participants at the lowest reasonable cost. This chapter will show you how to bring together the various elements needed to achieve this goal.

Your participants' ability to retire successfully is directly tied to how much they save, the returns they earn, and the amount they pay. Therefore, the foundation of the ideal plan is built upon these three pillars:

- Effective Plan Design
- Successful Investment Experiences
- Cost Containment

Choosing Service Providers

I strongly believe that building the ideal 401(k) plan is best accomplished using an "unbundled" approach and begins with choosing the right service providers. Members of the team should include:

- Independent, Registered Investment Advisor (RIA)
- Independent Record-keeper/Third-Party Administrator

- Custodian/Trustee
- Auditor (if applicable)
- ERISA attorney (if applicable)

Designing the Plan

The key to designing an ideal plan is to make it automatic. This includes automatically enrolling employees, automatically increasing their deferrals each year, and automatically investing each participant into a "qualified default investment alternative" or QDIA.

With automatic enrollment, the plan sponsor needs to make a couple of important decisions. First, should it only apply to new hires or retroactively to all employees? To achieve the best results, make it applicable to all employees. They can always opt-out if they do not want to participate. Second, the plan sponsor needs to select a "default" beginning deferral rate between 3 and 10 percent. Prudent fiduciaries recognize that modest deferral rates will not lead to adequate or meaningful retirement benefits. I recommend the default deferral rate be in the 4 to 8 percent range (the higher the better).

To retire successfully, a good rule of thumb is that participants should be saving at least 10 to 15 percent of their income each year through a combination of their own deferrals plus employer contributions. Automatically increasing deferrals each year helps participants achieve this target incrementally over time. A good approach is to increase deferral rates by 2 percent each year. Assuming the default deferral rate was 4 percent, an employee who remains in the plan and does not opt-out of the plan or the increases would be contributing 10 percent of her income after three years. If the employer contributes 3 percent in the form of matching or profit-sharing, the employee will be saving 13 percent of her income and well on her way to a successful retirement.

Lastly, automatically enrolled employees should be defaulted into a qualified default investment alternative (QDIA) that is suitable for long-term retirement savings. As previously mentioned there are three main types of QDIAs —lifestyle or life-cycle/target-retirement date funds, balanced funds, and managed accounts. Each is different in its composition and approach but they all have the same benefit—broad diversification and professional management. These two elements are critical for successful investment experiences.

Regardless of which QDIA approach that is selected, it is important to design the plan in a way that participants utilize the QDIA correctly. Since a QDIA is designed to be a "one-stop-shop" investment approach, the plan should ensure that all employee contributions go strictly into the selected QDIA.

Unfortunately, studies have shown that the average participant who invests in a lifestyle fund also holds a total of 4.8 additional funds in his or her account.[1] This defeats the purpose of utilizing the lifestyle fund (or other QDIA) and potentially subjects the participant to too much or too little risk. The only way to solve this problem is to make it an all-or-nothing proposition and require the participants who select a QDIA to invest all their money in this option. Plan sponsors should work with their 401(k) provider to ensure this approach can be implemented.

Selecting the Investments

In Chapter 5, I highlighted the fact that most plan participants are ill-equipped to make their own investment decisions. To deliver successful investment experiences for the participants, the ideal 401(k) plan should utilize an independent, Registered Investment Advisor (RIA) who accepts discretion over plan assets and serves as an ERISA §3(38) "investment manager."

The investment manager, serving as an independent

fiduciary, takes the responsibility for developing the investment policy for the plan, selects which asset classes will be represented, and determines the specific investments for each asset class. For the greatest diversification and long-term performance benefits, the plan should include asset classes such as small stocks, international stocks, emerging markets stocks, real estate, and commodities.

Once these decisions have been made, the investment manager creates model portfolios which participants can select based upon their risk tolerance, time horizon, and return requirements. The investment manager is then responsible for monitoring the portfolio allocations and following a disciplined, prudent process for making investment decisions.

As previously stated, this professionally managed approach not only benefits the plan sponsor through the transfer of fiduciary responsibility, it should also deliver better returns over time for plan participants. To contain costs, the plan should primarily consist of low-cost passively managed investments rather than actively managed funds. Chapter 5 outlines the rationale for a passively managed approach.

It is important to note that this approach may not initially be popular with some employees, so you need to effectively communicate the changes and explain the reasons for the changes. In the real world, there are always a handful of participants who will passionately argue against this approach because they perceive it as taking away their individual right to self-direct. While the majority of participants will likely appreciate and want to use the model portfolio approach, the complaints of those few "squeaky wheels" can make life difficult for the plan decision-makers.

At its core, an ERISA-governed retirement plan is a trust and the plan fiduciaries have a duty to administer the plan in the best interest of the beneficiaries (i.e. participants). Remembering that the role of a fiduciary is to make decisions for the exclusive purpose of providing retirement benefits, plan fiduciaries should focus on the needs of many rather than the wishes of a few. While a small percentage of retirement plan participants may be capable of making good investment decisions for themselves, the vast majority are not. In essence, a plan fiduciary is like a parent and sometimes the best thing that can be done for a child is also the hardest thing at the time. Similarly, although the decision to design a plan this way will not be popular with everyone, it will likely produce the best results for the participants as a whole. Special care should be taken to develop an effective communication strategy for participants and to take the necessary time to answer their questions. Approached correctly, this type of retirement plan has the chance to earn the goodwill and appreciation of participants, especially as they begin to see its effectiveness. In time, I believe your participants will thank you as they begin to see themselves and their colleagues retire with meaningful, and likely, substantial retirement benefits.

Paying for Services

Too few plan sponsors evaluate their plans from a total cost of ownership perspective. The ideal 401(k) plan minimizes asset-based fees (see Chapter 7) and requires every service provider to fully disclose its fees in an easy-to-understand fashion. The independent Registered Investment Advisor is generally the professional who is most qualified to drive this process for the plan sponsor.

Asset-based fees should be charged by the funds in the plan, but these fees should be low if passive investments are being utilized. The weighted average of the plan's model portfolios (using passively managed funds) should be less than one-half of one percent. The RIA, if serving as an "investment manager" will also likely charge an asset-based, investment advisory fee which should range from 0.1 to 0.5 percent. Lastly, most custodians charge an asset-based fee (usually .15 percent or lower) for their services.

The independent record-keeper should bill their services on a per-participant basis and may require a "base fee" or minimum fee for their services. They should receive no asset-based fees for their services and any revenue sharing they receive should be credited back to the plan to offset their directly billed charges. If the plan has more than 100 participants and requires an audit, an accounting firm should be hired. Fees will vary depending upon the scope of the engagement but should be billed as a flat fee, a retainer, or on an hourly basis. The same method of compensation should be used if the plan requires the services of an ERISA attorney.

While fees for each service provider will vary, here is an example of what it could cost using the example of a $5,000,000 plan with 100 employees:

Asset Class	Assets	Assets	Fund	Exp.	Cost
US Large Cap	$750,000	15.00%	Vanguard Large Cap Index	0.20%	$1,500.00
US Small Cap	$750,000	15.00%	Vanguard Small Cap Index	0.22%	$1,650.00
International Large	$750,000	15.00%	Vanguard Developed Markets Index Fund	0.22%	$1,650.00
Emerging Market	$150,000	3.00%	Vanguard Emerging Markets Stock Index	0.22%	$330.00
US Bonds	$1,250,000	25.00%	Vanguard Short Term Bond Index	0.18%	$2,250.00
International Bonds	$500,000	10.00%	Fidelity New Markets Income Fund	0.90%	$4,500.00
Real Estate	$600,000	12.00%	Vanguard REIT	0.21%	$1,260.00
Cash	$250,000	5.00%	Vanguard Prime Money Market	0.29%	$725.00
Total Assets	$5,000,000	100.00%			
Weighted Average Expense Ratio (Participant Paid)				0.28%	$13,865.00
RIA Advisory Fee (Participant Paid)				0.40%	$20,000.00
Custodian Fees (Participant Paid)				0.10%	$5,000.00
Trustee Fees (Employer Paid)				0.02%	$1,000.00
Administration Fees (Employer Paid)				0.14%	$7,000.00
TOTAL PARTICIPANT FEES				**0.78%**	**$38,865.00**
TOTAL EMPLOYER FEES				**0.16%**	**$8,000.00**

In this scenario, the average participant cost is .78 percent of assets and is comprised of three separate fees which can be considered the participant's "investment expenses":

- ***Weighted Average Expense Ratio***: This is the weighted average of the expense ratios for each fund in the plan.
- ***RIA Advisory Fee:*** This is the asset-based fee charged by the ERISA §3(38) investment manager for discretionary investment advisory services.
- ***Custodian Fee:*** This fee compensates the custodian for providing back-office functions such as cash receipt and disbursement functions, trading, and mutual fund settlement services.

This represents tremendous value for the participant and the likelihood of much greater retirement accumulation considering the industry average investment expenses for a plan this size is 1.27 percent.[2] That equates to a cost savings of nearly 40 percent. As plan assets grow, the RIA advisory fee may decrease from a relative percentage standpoint, depending upon the fee structure of the RIA.

In this example, the costs for administration are paid directly by the employer although it is possible they could be assessed to the participants. These costs work out to $70 per participant, which represents .14 percent of plan assets ($7,000 divided by $5,000,000). Since these fees are explicitly billed rather than asset-based, they can be easily contained over time. Unless the number of participants increases, these costs should remain fairly stable over time and go down as a percentage of assets as the plan grows.

Except for the very smallest plans, an ideal 401(k) plan should have total fees that range from .65 percent to 1.50 percent, excluding auditor and/or attorney fees. In addition, eliminating asset-based fees for recordkeeping and administration will drive these fees even lower.

Conclusion

Implementing an ideal 401(k) plan is what plan participants deserve (and need) to retire with meaningful benefits and is easily attainable for the well-informed plan sponsor. However, it requires knowledgeable plan fiduciaries who are committed to prudently selecting their service providers, holding them accountable, and measuring their effectiveness.

Questions To Ask:

1. Does my plan look like the "ideal" or something else?
2. Have I focused on designing my plan with the three pillars of success in mind or something else?
3. What changes do I need consider to make my plan "ideal"?

CHAPTER 12

A Case Study

This final chapter demonstrates the significant economic value that an ideal 401(k) plan can create for employees—the ability to accumulate meaningful and substantial benefits and retire successfully. Let us compare two "average" employees at similar companies, Jim Smith and Bill Johnson. Jim works for Company A which has a "typical" 401(k) plan while Bill works for Company B which has an "ideal" 401(k) plan. Both Jim and Bill are age thirty-five, make $75,000 per year, have an account balance of $66,650[1], and make $7,500 in annual contributions between salary deferral and company matching.

Jim's Story

Jim's plan (Company A) utilizes a non-fiduciary "financial advisor" who has recommended actively managed funds for the plan which are all well-known and considered "good" or "excellent" funds by various media outlets and mutual fund rating agencies. Unfortunately, the plan fiduciaries for the company are unaware that mutual funds come in different share classes which can have a dramatic effect on the cost to the participants. Since the financial advisor is a non-fiduciary and is paid to "sell" retirement plans, he has never discussed these cost differences and the plan includes higher cost share classes.

The financial advisor provides an "education" meeting

each year for the employees but does not provide any specific investment advice or recommendations to the participants. It is Jim's responsibility to "build" his own portfolio using the funds provided in the plan. For his services, the financial advisor is paid by the mutual funds in the plan through 12b-1 fees (i.e., commissions) although neither the plan fiduciaries nor the participants are quite sure how much compensation he receives. In reality, the financial advisor is making over $35,000 per year from the plan and has certain funds because that pay him a higher commission than similar, less expensive options. Although he struggles with this conflict of interest from time to time, his firm (a major Wall Street brokerage) puts a lot of pressure on him to get his sales numbers up and he simply does what he has to. Besides, in his mind, an additional .50 percent or so will not make a big difference to the participants over time.

Jim has over thirty different investment options in his plan which he finds very confusing, and, although he is not a sophisticated investor, he recognizes the names of many of the funds in his plan and has been impressed by the number of "stars" most have received from Morningstar. He chooses the following funds from his options:

Asset Class	Fund (Share Class)	Expense Ratio
US Large Cap Equity	Legg Mason Value Trust	1.68%
US Small Cap Equity	Royce Total Return (Consultant Class)	2.07%
International Equity	American Funds Europacific Growth (R-2)	1.59%
Emerging Markets Equity	American Funds New World (R-2)	1.80%
US Bonds	American Funds Bond Fund of America (R-2)	1.41%
International Bonds	MainStay Global High Income A	1.40%
Real Estate	AIM Real Estate R	1.52%
Cash	Management Trust of America (R-2)	1.44%
Average Fund Expense		**1.60%**

Jim does his best to build his own "portfolio" using the funds in the plan and tends to select those that have had the best performance over the past one and three year time periods. The average annual investment expense for his portfolio is 1.60 percent although he has had a hard time figuring this out because the fees are not fully disclosed. Admittedly, he makes few changes and only looks at the account about once per year, although when the stock market becomes very volatile he takes the "safe" approach and transfers his balance into the cash fund. Once the market recovers he usually reinvests his money when he gets an opportunity, although he sometimes fails to do so in a timely fashion because of work and family commitments.

Jim maintains his savings and investment approach over the course of his career and earns a 5.3 percent average annual return which enables him to accumulate over $585,000 in retirement assets (see chart below).

Year	Retirement Savings
Year 1	$77,473
Year 5	$122,471
Year 10	$188,742
Year 15	$268,214
Year 20	$363,517
Year 25	$477,806
Year 30	$585,423

After thirty years, Jim decides to retire at age sixty-five and uses his 401(k) balance to purchase an immediate fixed-income annuity that guarantees him $4,092 per month in income for the rest of his life.[2] This combined with his Social Security of $1,500 per month enables Jim to generate over $67,000 in yearly retirement income, which is slightly more than the $60,000 he needs to live. Although he is glad to be retired, his experience is not entirely what he expected. He finds that he cannot do all the things he wanted to during his "Golden Years" simply because money is too tight. When costs rise, he often finds himself considering a part-time job to ease the pressure.

Bill's Story

Bill's plan (Company B) takes a different approach than Jim's. Company B's plan fiduciaries are savvy and well-informed as to their fiduciary duties. After a thorough due diligence process, they select and appoint a Registered Investment Advisor (RIA) as an ERISA §3(38) "investment manager" and §405(d)(1) "independent fiduciary" to professionally manage the plan assets on a discretionary basis. To fulfill their duties under ERISA, the plan fiduciaries also meet with the RIA each quarter to review and monitor its performance.

Based on significant amounts of research and real world experience, the investment manager believes a passive approach to investing is most prudent and cost effective. Using mostly low-cost index funds, the investment manager designs four different "portfolios" for participants to invest in based on their time horizon, risk tolerance, and expected return requirements. The investment manager builds these portfolios using the funds on the following page:

These portfolios take the guesswork out of the investing process since they are already pre-diversified and serve as a single investment strategy for each participant. Since Bill is not a sophisticated investor, he really appreciates the fact that he simply has to select which portfolio is most appropriate for his stage of life. He also likes that the average fund expense in his plan is .30 percent, although the weighted expense of his "portfolio" is only .28 percent. Bill and the rest of the participants also pay .10 percent to the custodian of the plan for its services.

Bill finds that he experiences much less stress and worry when he thinks about his 401(k) account because he knows a professional independent fiduciary is managing the process

Asset Class	Fund (Share Class)	Expense Ratio
US Large Cap Equity	Vanguard Large Cap Index	0.20%
US Small Cap Equity	Vanguard Small Cap Index	0.22%
International Equity	Vanguard Developed Markets Index Fund	0.22%
Emerging Markets Equity	Vanguard Emerging Markets Stock Index	0.22%
US Fixed Bonds	Vanguard Short Term Bond Index	0.18%
International Bonds	Fidelity New Markets Income Fund	0.90%
Real Estate	Vanguard REIT	0.21%
Cash	Vanguard Prime Money Market	0.29%
Average Fund Expense		**0.30%**

for him and his fellow workers. It also enables him to focus more clearly on work and on spending time with his family. While the gyrations of the market give him pause from time to time, he has seen how a disciplined and diversified approach weathers the storm. In fact, at one point during the past year his portfolio was only down three percent while the S&P 500 was down nearly ten percent over the same period of time. Over time, he finds these experiences make it easier to stay the course during the inevitable ups and downs of the market.

For its services, the investment manager receives an annual fee of .40 percent which equates to $20,000 in compensation from the plan (prorated and deducted across participant accounts.) This fee is charged each quarter and is fully disclosed to the plan via an invoice and to participants on their account statements. Although the firm recognizes it could charge higher fees and earn greater profits by "selling" certain types of 401(k) products, they are satisfied their fees provide a reasonable profit for the services they provide to the plan and its participants. The plan fiduciaries agree and appreciate the investment manager's approach to full and easy-to-understand disclosure of fees. It also helps that the investment manager is an independent firm that is accountable solely to clients as opposed to a publicly-traded firm that has to answer to shareholders above all else.

With total portfolio expenses of .78 percent, Bill is confident he is getting tremendous value from his 401(k) plan. His former company had a low quality, high cost plan that made it seem like his account balance never grew the way it should. He and many of his co-workers periodically share how much they appreciate working for a company that cares so much about helping them retire with meaningful benefits.

Bill maintains his savings and investment approach over the course of his career and earns a 7.2 percent average annual return due to the disciplined and diversified strategy utilized by the investment manager. Unlike Jim, the investment manager does not make poor investment decisions driven by emotion which contributes to Bill earning a higher return. This enables Bill to accumulate over $1,000,000 in retirement assets (see chart below).

Year	Retirement Savings
Year 1	$79,505
Year 5	$137,108
Year 10	$232,517
Year 15	$362,745
Year 20	$540,499
Year 25	$783,125
Year 30	$1,039,574

After thirty years, Bill decides to retire at age sixty-five and uses his 401(k) balance to purchase an immediate fixed-income annuity that guarantees him $7,267 per month in income for the rest of his life.[3] This combined with his Social Security of $1,500 per month enables Jim to generate over

$105,000 in yearly retirement income, which is significantly more than the $60,000 he needs to live comfortably. He even finds that he ***saves*** money each year!

Retirement is everything that Bill expected it to be. He travels often, plays quite a bit of golf, and has even started volunteering at a non-profit organization he has supported for many years. While many of his retired friends have resorted to working part-time, he is thankful this is not a consideration for him.

Conclusion

Similar stories with very different outcomes (over $450,000 in difference to be exact). Is your 401(k) plan more like Company A or Company B? Which company do you think your employees would rather work for?

As a plan fiduciary, you have the opportunity to make an incredible impact on the lives of your employees and their families. You can increase the likelihood that your participants will have a terrific retirement experience instead of a terrifying one, simply by making well-informed, prudent decisions for your plan. I hope this book has helped you grasp the critical importance of your responsibility, shown you ways you can fulfill your duties more effectively, and motivated you to take action. The rest is up to you and the time is now. Good luck!

Appendix 1

Disclosure Concerning Potential Conflicts Of Interest

This disclosure form is reprinted with permission of Pete Swisher and Unified Trust Company, N.A.

Introduction

Qualified plan fiduciaries are obligated to ensure that costs paid for services to the plan are reasonable and to discover the full extent of all compensation paid to service providers. Fiduciaries are prohibited under ERISA Section 406 from actions which represent a conflict between self-interest and the interests of the plan participants and beneficiaries. A prudent fiduciary requires disclosure of any potential conflicts of interest affecting its service providers.

The purpose of this document is twofold:

- To obtain complete disclosure of all compensation, however derived, of current and potential service providers of:________________________ (plan name), and;
- To make clear all possible conflicts of interest affecting current and potential service providers regardless of fiduciary status.

Instructions

Please complete and sign this form on your company's behalf. If you wish you may attach explanatory material in support of your answers.

Service Provider Information

Service Provider Company Name:

____

Name of person completing this form:

____

Title: ______________________________

Nature of services to be provided (check all that apply):

- ☐ Recordkeeper
- ☐ Administrator
- ☐ Investment Advisor (including advice provider)
- ☐ ERISA Investment Manager
- ☐ Consultant providing fiduciary oversight or other services
- ☐ Custodian
- ☐ Trustee
- ☐ Brokerage/securities sales
- ☐ Money management

Disclosures

1. ***Proprietary Investments*** (check all that apply)
   - ☐ Provider offers proprietary investment products
   - ☐ Provider requires that a certain percentage of plan investment options or assets be invested in Vendor's proprietary products
   - ☐ Provider offers a GIC and may draw revenue, directly or indirectly, from assets invested in this GIC

2. **Compensation Disclosure** (check all that apply)
   - ☐ Provider is paid fees or commissions for its services, the full amounts of which have been disclosed to the client
   - ☐ Yes ☐ No Provider further certifies that the disclosed fees or commissions are the sole source of compensation for Provider.
   - ☐ Provider is paid fees or commissions for its services, the full amounts of which have not been disclosed to the client
   - ☐ Provider is revenue neutral, meaning that provider receives neither more nor less compensation regardless of the investments selected
   - ☐ Provider is not revenue neutral, meaning that in the selection of investments to be offered to the client, the provider may draw higher revenues from some investments than from others (such as in the form of revenue sharing payments)
   - ☐ Vendor or vendor's affiliate/subsidiary is paid transaction-based commissions for one or more transactions on behalf of the client
   - ☐ Vendor pays or receives deposit-based commissions or fees, including payments on transfer amounts (e.g., finders' fees)

- ☐ Vendor (or related entity) receives and keeps compensation from the following sources, or pays such compensation to other parties in connection with qualified plan services: (check all that apply)
- ☐ Commissions on investment products
- ☐ Fees for service
- ☐ Sub-transfer agency fees
- ☐ Shareholder servicing fees
- ☐ Finder's fees and/or 12(b)(1) fees
- ☐ Soft dollar arrangements
- ☐ Money manager fee-sharing
- ☐ Placement fees (such as "preferred vendor" fees)
- ☐ Transaction-based commissions
- ☐ Dealer spreads
- ☐ Other

3. Have the full amounts of all compensation named above been disclosed to the client in a clear and understandable format?
   - ☐ Yes
   - ☐ No

4. **Revenue Sharing** (check one)
   - ☐ "Aetna Model" (DOL AO 97-16A)—provider keeps some or all payments from investment companies (check all that apply)
   - ☐ Vendor has not disclosed or will not disclose the full dollar amounts of all revenue sharing payments it collects

- ☐ Vendor provides full disclosure of amounts of revenue sharing collected in connection with each investment
- ☐ Vendor offsets its fees with revenue sharing payments but keeps any revenue sharing payments in excess of its fees
- ☐ "Frost Model" (DOL AO 97-15A)—provider passes back to the plan 100% of all revenue sharing payments and accounts for these payments to the plan sponsor no less than annually

5. **Revenue Sharing accounting**
   - ☐ Vendor's accounting system tracks revenue sharing payments vs. anticipated/expected payments and how such payments are applied
   - ☐ Vendor provides reports to plan sponsor showing amounts of revenue sharing and how applied. Reports are provided:
     - ☐ Quarterly
     - ☐ Annually
     - ☐ Other:____________________________

6. **Soft dollars** (check all that apply)
   - ☐ Vendor accepts or makes soft dollar arrangements in connection with retirement plan clients (such as providing or accepting research or other services). Explain:____________________________

     ____
   - ☐ Vendor does not disclose the nature or value of such arrangements
   - ☐ Vendor does disclose the nature or value of such arrangements

7. ***Revenue from related entities*** (check all that apply)

☐ Provider owns or is affiliated with or has an interest in one or more entities that may draw revenue as a consequence of vendor's provision of service to the client (for example, a self-clearing broker/dealer's trading subsidiary may be paid for executing transactions). Explain:____________________

____

☐ The vendor's owners or employees may benefit from the vendor's provision of service to the client through entities in which the owners' or employees' relatives have an interest. Explain:

____

____

Certification and Signature

I affirm that I am authorized to complete this document on behalf of ____________________(company) and that all answers are a true and complete representation of the services rendered by my company.

________________________________(signature)

Date:____________________________

Appendix 2

Selecting and Monitoring Pension Consultants - Tips for Plan Fiduciaries

The following information is from the Department of Labor. It can also be found at http://www.dol.gov/ebsa.

Background

The Employee Retirement Income Security Act (ERISA) requires that fiduciaries of employee benefit plans administer and manage their plans prudently and in the interest of the plan's participants and beneficiaries. In carrying out these responsibilities, plan fiduciaries often rely heavily on pension consultants and other professionals for help. Findings included in a report by the staff of the U.S. Securities and Exchange Commission released in May 2005, however, raise serious questions concerning whether some pension consultants are fully disclosing potential conflicts of interest that may affect the objectivity of the advice they are providing to their pension plan clients.

Under the Investment Advisers Act of 1940 (Advisers Act), an investment adviser providing consulting services has a fiduciary duty to provide disinterested advice and disclose any material conflicts of interest to their clients. In this context, SEC staff examined the practices of advisers that provide pension consulting services to plan sponsors and fiduciaries. These consulting services included assisting in determining the plans investment objectives and restrictions, allocating plan assets, selecting money managers, choosing mutual fund options, tracking investment performance, and selecting other service providers. Many of the consultants also offered, directly or through an affiliate or subsidiary, products and services to money managers. Additionally, many of the consultants also offered, directly or through an affiliate or subsidiary, brokerage and money management services, often marketed to plans as a package of bundled services. The SEC examination staff concluded in its report that the business alliances among pension consultants and money managers can give rise to serious potential conflicts of interest under the Advisers Act that need to be monitored and disclosed to plan fiduciaries.

To encourage the disclosure and review of more and better information about potential conflicts of interest, the Department of Labor and the SEC have developed the following set of questions to assist plan fiduciaries in evaluating the objectivity of the recommendations provided, or to be provided, by a pension consultant.

1. **Are you registered with the SEC or a state securities regulator as an investment adviser? If so, have you provided me with all the disclosures required under those laws (including Part II of Form ADV)?**

   You can check yourself - and view the firm's Form ADV - by searching the SEC's Investment Adviser Public Disclosure Web site. At present, the IAPD database contains Forms ADV only for investment adviser firms that register electronically using the Investment Adviser Registration Depository. In the future, the database will expand to encompass all registered investment advisers - individuals as well as firms - in every state. If you can't locate an investment adviser in IAPD, be sure to contact your state securities regulator or the SEC's Public Reference Branch.

2. **Do you or a related company have relationships with money managers that you recommend, consider for recommendation, or otherwise mention to the plan? If so, describe those relationships.**

   When pension consultants have alliances or financial or other relationships with money managers or other service providers, the potential for material conflicts of interest increases depending on the extent of the relationships. Knowing what relationships, if any, your pension consultant has with money managers may help you assess the objectivity of the advice the consultant provides.

3. **Do you or a related company receive any payments from money managers you recommend, consider for recommendation, or otherwise mention to the plan for our consideration? If so, what is the extent of these payments in relation to your other income (revenue)?**

   Payments from money managers to pension consultants could create material conflicts of interests. You may wish to assess the extent of potential conflicts.

4. **Do you have any policies or procedures to address conflicts of interest or to prevent these payments or relationships from being a factor when you provide advice to your clients?**

   Probing how the consultant addresses these potential conflicts may help you determine whether the consultant is right for your plan.

5. **If you allow plans to pay your consulting fees using the plan's brokerage commissions, do you monitor the amount of commissions paid and alert plans when consulting fees have been paid in full? If not, how can a plan make sure it does not over-pay its consulting fees?**

   You may wish to avoid any payment arrangements that could cause the plan to pay more than it should in pension consultant fees.

6. **If you allow plans to pay your consulting fees using the plan's brokerage commissions, what steps do you take to ensure that the plan receives best execution for its securities trades?**

   Where and how brokerage orders are executed can impact the overall costs of the transaction, including the price the plan pays for the securities it purchases.

7. **Do you have any arrangements with broker-dealers under which you or a related company will benefit if money managers place trades for their clients with such broker-dealers?**

   As noted above, you may wish to explore the consultants' relationships with other service providers to weigh the extent of any potential conflicts of interest.

8. **If you are hired, will you acknowledge in writing that you have a fiduciary obligation as an investment adviser to the plan while providing the consulting services we are seeking?**

   All investment advisers (whether registered with the SEC or not) owe their advisory clients a fiduciary duty. Among other things, this means that advisers must disclose to their clients information about material conflicts of interest.

9. **Do you consider yourself a fiduciary under ERISA with respect to the recommendations you provide the plan?**

   If the consultant is a fiduciary under ERISA and receives fees from third parties as a result of their recommendations, a prohibited transaction under ERISA occurs unless the fees are used for the benefit of the plan (e.g., offset against the consulting fees charged the plan) or there is a relevant exemption.

10. **What percentage of your plan clients utilize money managers, investment funds, brokerage services or other service providers from whom you receive fees?**

    The answer may help in evaluating the objectivity of the recommendations or the fiduciary status of the consultant under ERISA.

For more information on the SEC staff's findings, please read "Staff Report Concerning Examinations Of Select Pension Consultants". Plan fiduciaries, pension consultants, and other service providers can learn about their fiduciary responsibilities under the Employee Retirement Income Security Act (ERISA) by visiting the Web site of the U.S. Department of Labor. Pension consultants who have questions concerning their obligations under the Investment Advisers Act of 1940 should either consult with an attorney who specializes in the federal securities laws or contact the staff of the SEC's Division of Investment Management.

This fact sheet has been developed by the U.S. Department of Labor, Employee Benefits Security Administration, Washington, DC 20210. It will be made available in alternate formats upon request: Voice phone: 202.693.8664;

TTY: 202.501.3911. In addition, the information in this fact sheet constitutes a small entity compliance guide for purposes of the Small Business Regulatory Enforcement Fairness Act of 1996.

APPENDIX 3

Tips for Selecting and Monitoring Service Providers for Your Employee Benefit Plan

The following information is from the Department of Labor. It can also be found at http://www.dol.gov/ebsa.

As sponsors of 401(k) and other types of pension plans, business owners generally are responsible for ensuring that their plans comply with Federal law – including the Employee Retirement Income Security Act (ERISA). Many businesses rely on other professionals to advise them and assist them with their employee benefit plan duties. For this reason, selecting competent service providers is one of the most important responsibilities of a plan sponsor. The process of selecting service providers will vary depending on the plan and services to be provided. To assist business owners in carrying out their responsibilities under ERISA to prudently select and monitor plan service providers, the Employee Benefits Security Administration has prepared the following tips which may be a helpful starting point:

1. Consider what services you need for your plan – legal, accounting, trustee/custodial, recordkeeping, investment management, investment education or advice.

2. Ask service providers about their services, experience with employee benefit plans, fees and expenses, customer references or other information relating to the quality of their services and customer satisfaction with such services.

3. Present each prospective service provider identical and complete information regarding the needs of your plan. You may want to get formal bids from those providers that seem best suited to your needs.

4. You may also wish to consider service providers or alliances of providers who provide multiple services (e.g., custodial trustee, investment management, education, or advice, and recordkeeping) for a single fee. These arrangements are often called "bundled services."

5. Ask each prospective provider to be specific about which services are covered for the estimated fees and which are not. Compare the information you receive, including fees and expenses to be charged by the various providers for similar services. Note that plan fiduciaries are not always required to pick the least costly provider. Cost is only one factor to be considered in selecting a service provider. More information on pension plan fees and expenses can be found in *Understanding Retirement Plan Fees and Expenses* and the *401(k) Fee Disclosure Form,* located at www.dol.gov/ebsa.

6. If the service provider will handle plan assets, check to make sure that the provider has a fidelity bond (a type of insurance that protects the plan against loss resulting from fraudulent or dishonest acts).

7. If a service provider must be licensed (attorneys, accountants, investment managers or advisors), check

with state or federal licensing authorities to confirm the provider has an up-to-date license and whether there are any complaints pending against the provider.

8. Make sure you understand the terms of any agreements or contracts you sign with service providers and the fees and expenses associated with the contracts. In particular, understand what obligations both you and the service provider have under the agreement and whether the fees and expenses to be charged to you and plan participants are reasonable in light of the services to be provided.
9. Prepare a written record of the process you followed in reviewing potential service providers and the reasons for your selection of a particular provider. This record may be helpful in answering any future questions that may arise concerning your selection.
10. Receive a commitment from your service provider to regularly provide you with information regarding the services it provides.
11. Periodically review the performance of your service providers to ensure that they are providing the services in a manner and at a cost consistent with the agreements.
12. Review plan participant comments or any complaints about the services and periodically ask whether there have been any changes in the information you received from the service provider prior to hiring (e.g. does the provider continue to maintain any required state or Federal licenses).

APPENDIX 4

Sample Fiduciary Audit File

Creating and maintaining a Fiduciary Audit File is a critical step to being a well-organized plan fiduciary. It serves as the central location for all plan related information and provides the "proof" that a prudent process for decision-making was followed. This file should be stored in both hard copy and electronic formats and be updated on a regular basis. Listed below is the file structure we use for our clients to help them easily categorize relevant information. These sections could serve as tabs in a binder or folders on a hard drive. Under each section are examples of the types of information that could be found.

Fiduciary Information

- Executed copy of the plan's Plan Oversight Committee Charter that lists the plan fiduciaries, their individual roles as they relate to the plan, the role of the committee in general, and the process for decision-making
- Executed copies of fiduciary acknowledgement letters by each plan fiduciary accepting their fiduciary status
- Documentation (handouts, presentations, etc.) of any annual fiduciary training that has been provided for plan fiduciaries

Fees & Expenses

- Invoices
- Any fee audit or analysis that has been conducted on the plan
- Fee disclosures provided by all service providers to the plan (each provider should provide their previous year compensation in both percentages and dollars on an annual basis, including direct and indirect compensation)
- Share class information

Plan Reviews

- 3-5 Year Strategic Plan
- Plan performance reviews
- Any benchmarking studies that have been conducted on the plan. These studies may provide analysis about issues such as plan design, employee participation/utilization, fiduciary issues, asset allocation/ investment diversity/investment monitoring, employee education, or total plan costs

Service Provider Documents

- Any contracts, agreements or engagement letters signed with the RIA, broker, custodian, recordkeeper, TPA, auditor, attorney, etc.
- Background information and due diligence reports for each service provider
- Annual Form ADV
- Fidelity bond coverage

Fund Information

- Mutual fund prospectus'
- Fund fact sheets

Investment Policy Statement

- The current version of the plan's Investment Policy Statement (IPS)
- Any historical copies of the plan's IPS

Investment Monitoring Reports

- Quarterly reports that analyze and monitor the plan investments according to the IPS

Meeting Minutes

- Minutes for every meeting that takes place regarding the plan. Minutes should include detailed information for any decisions that have been made and the reasoning behind these decisions

Employee Education & Enrollment

- Copies of any information (handouts, presentations, risk tolerance questionnaires, etc.) that has been used to educate plan participants
- Enrollment forms

Plan Documents

- Plan document
- Adoption agreement
- Summary Plan Description (SPD)
- Designation of beneficiary forms

- 404(c) notice
- Safe Harbor notice (if applicable)
- QDIA, EACA, or QACA notices

Appendix 5

20 Steps to 404(c) Compliance

This checklist is reprinted with permission of Fred Reish from Reish, Luftman, Reicher & Cohen.

The participant has an opportunity to obtain written confirmation of his instructions

- The person to whom the instructions are given is an identified plan fiduciary who is obligated to comply with the instructions
- The participant is provided by an identified plan fiduciary with the following:
    1. An explanation that the plan is intended to be a 404(c) plan;
    2. An explanation that the fiduciaries of the plan may be relieved of liability for losses;
    3. A description of the investment alternatives available under the plan;
    4. A general description of the investment objectives and risk and return characteristics of each designated alternative;
    5. Identification of any designated investment managers;
    6. An explanation about giving investment instructions;

7. A description of any transaction fees and expenses which affect the participant's account balance;
8. The name, address, and phone number of the plan fiduciary responsible for providing information;
9. Specified information regarding employer securities;
10. A copy of the most recent prospectus provided to the plan for investment alternatives subject to the Securities Act of 1933;
11. Any materials provided to the plan relating to the exercise of voting, tender or similar rights.

- The participant is able to obtain upon request:

1. A description of the annual operating expenses of each designated investment alternative;
2. Copies of any prospectuses, financial statements and reports provided to the plan;
3. A list of the assets comprising the portfolio of each designated investment alternative;
4. Information concerning the value of shares or units in designated investment alternatives;
5. Information concerning the value of shares or units in designated investment alternatives held in the account of the participant.
6. Plan permits participants to give investment instructions with a frequency which is appropriate in light of market volatility.
7. The core investment alternatives, constituting a broad range, permit instructions at least once within any three-month period.

Glossary of Terms

401(k): A type of employer-sponsored defined contribution retirement plan under section 401(k) of the Internal Revenue Code that allows a worker to save for retirement while deferring income taxes on any contributions and earnings until withdrawal.

12b-1 fee: Also known as a "trailing commission," this fee is paid by a mutual fund out of fund assets to cover distribution expenses and sometimes shareholder service expenses. In most cases, it serves as a commission used to compensate brokers and others who sell fund shares to 401(k) participants. 12b-1 fees generally range from .25 percent to 1 percent depending upon the mutual fund and share class.

Active Management: The art of stock picking and market timing where fund managers and investors rely on analytical research and their own judgment in making investment decisions on what securities to buy, hold, and sell. Active managers attempt to outperform a benchmark index which is the opposite of passive management, generally known as "indexing".

Administrative Fees: One time, event-driven fees that are charged directly to participants for services such as processing distribution and loan requests.

Asset Class: A group of securities with shared economic traits, such as stocks, bonds, real estate, or cash.

Asset-Based Fee: A fee charged by a service provider to underwrite the cost of services to a retirement plan and based on a percentage of plan assets.

Auditor: Federal law requires employee benefit plans with 100 or more participants to have an audit as part of their obligation to file an annual return/report (known as the Form 5500). By law, an auditor engaged for an employee benefit plan audit must be licensed or certified as a public accountant by a State regulatory authority.

Automatic Deferral Increase: A 401(k) feature highlighted in the Pension Protection Act of 2006 which automatically schedules future increases to a participant's salary deferral rate established at enrollment. Participants may opt-out of these increases at any time.

Automatic Enrollment: A 401(k) feature highlighted in the Pension Protection Act of 2006 by which an employer can automatically enroll employees in the plan. Participants may opt-out of the plan at any time.

Baby Boomer Generation: A term used to describe a person born between 1946 and 1964.

Balanced Fund: A mutual fund which buys a combination of stocks, bonds, cash, and other investments. The purpose of a balanced fund is to provide investors with a single mutual fund that combines both growth and income objectives. A balanced fund is considered a "Qualified Default Investment Alternative" or QDIA under the Pension Protection Act of 2006.

Base Fee: An annual minimum fee charged by a recordkeeper or third-party administrator for services provided to a retirement plan. This fee is usually in addition to per participant fees and/or asset-based fees.

Basis Points: A unit that is equal to 1/100th of 1 percent, and is used to denote asset-based fees in the retirement plan industry. For instance, .25 percent is equal to 25 basis points.

Behavioral Finance: A field of finance which applies scientific research on human and social cognitive and emotional biases to better understand economic decisions and how they affect market prices, returns, and the allocation of resources.

Benchmark Index: A standard against which the performance of a security, mutual fund, or investment manager can be measured. For instance, the S&P 500 Index broadly measures the performance of U.S. large cap stocks.

Benefits Broker: A financial firm that typically provides a variety of products such as group life insurance, health and dental insurance, disability and long-term care insurance. Many of these companies also sell retirement plan products to employers as an ancillary benefit. Benefits providers are usually licensed brokers or registered representatives who represent a variety of insurance companies and most often sell insurance-based products such as group annuities.

Broker/Registered Representative: Generally, a non-fiduciary who acts as an intermediary between a buyer and seller, and usually receives a commission, such as a 12b-1 fee, for their services.

Broker-Dealer (B/D): A company that trades securities for both its customers (as a broker) and itself (as a dealer) and who is registered with the Financial Industry Regulatory Authority (FINRA). Brokers and registered representatives must be affiliated with a broker-dealer to transact business.

Bundled Provider: A single 401k vendor that provides all investment, recordkeeping, administration, and education services.

Capital Preservation Product: Under the PPA, a type of Qualified Default Investment Alternative (QDIA) that can only be used for the first 120 days after the date of the participant's first elective contribution. Examples are stable value or money market funds.

Co-Fiduciary: Relates to situations in which one plan fiduciary may be responsible for actions of another plan fiduciary. Some service providers tout "co-fiduciary" responsibility which may or may not provide a genuine transfer of fiduciary liability from the plan sponsor to the service provider, depending on discretion.

Conflicts of Interest: A situation in which someone in a position of trust has competing professional or personal interests which can make it difficult to fulfill his or her duties objectively. A conflict of interest exists even if no unethical or improper act results from it.

Consultant: A person who advises a plan sponsor or plan participants on matters related to the plan. The consultant may or may not serve in an acknowledged fiduciary capacity depending on the services they provide to the plan. This term can be used to describe a broker/registered representative or a Registered Investment Advisor (RIA).

Consulting Fee: A fully disclosed, flat fee charged by an advisory firm for providing consulting services to a retirement plan.

Surrender Charge: A penalty assessed by an insurance company if a customer terminates a variable group annuity within a specified number of years.

Contract Administrator: See "Third-Party Administrator (TPA)."

Cost Containment: The concept of minimizing asset-based fees in a retirement plan so as to reduce and control participant-paid fees over time.

Custodian: A financial institution that has the legal responsibility for a plan's assets and provides back-office functions such as cash receipt and disbursement functions, trading, and mutual fund settlement services.

Defined Benefit Plan: A plan that promises to pay a specified amount to each employee who retires after a set number of years of service. Also known as a pension or DB plan, contributions to the plan are made and managed by the employer.

Department of Labor (DOL): A Cabinet department of the United States government responsible for occupational safety, wage and hour standards, unemployment insurance benefits, re-employment services, and some economic statistics.

Direct Compensation: Any fully disclosed compensation received directly by a service provider from a company or retirement plan.

Directed Trustee: A directed trustee holds or safeguards custody of plan assets and takes direction from the plan sponsor. The plan sponsor must sign and approve all actions of the directed trustee.

Discretion: A person is a fiduciary with respect to a plan to the extent he or she exercises any discretionary authority or control over the management of the plan, or the management or disposition of plan assets or has any discretionary authority or responsibility in the administration of the plan.

Discretionary Corporate Trustee: A fully discretionary trustee takes sole responsibility for all aspects of plan assets. Appointing a discretionary trustee is a fiduciary act, and the plan sponsor must document and be able to demonstrate it was prudent in the selection and appointment of the discretionary trustee. When properly appointed, the fiduciary duties for plan investments will be allocated to the discretionary trustee and will relieve the plan sponsor and its employees of these responsibilities. The plan sponsor will retain only the obligation to prudently select and monitor the performance of the discretionary trustee.

Employee Benefits Security Administration (EBSA): A Department of Labor agency that oversees pension plans, health plans, and other employee benefits for more than 150 million people. EBSA is responsible for the administration and enforcement of Title I of the Employee Retirement Income Security Act of 1974 (ERISA).

Engagement Letter: A letter (or agreement) that defines the legal relationship (or engagement) between a professional firm and its client. This document states the terms and conditions of the engagement, specifically outlining the scope of the engagement and the terms of compensation for the firm.

The Employee Retirement Income Security Act of 1974 (ERISA): A federal law that sets minimum standards for most voluntarily established pension and health plans in private industry to provide protection for individuals in these plans.

 ERISA §3(16): This section of ERISA defines the term "administrator" to include the person specifically designated by the terms of the instrument under which the plan is operated, or if an administrator is not so designated, the plan sponsor. The plan administrator oversees the operation of the plan.

ERISA §3(21): This section of ERISA defines a fiduciary as anyone who exercises any discretionary authority or discretionary control respecting management of such plan or exercises any authority or control respecting management or disposition of its assets, has any discretionary authority or discretionary responsibility in the administration of such plan, or renders investment advice for a fee or other compensation, direct or indirect, with respect to any moneys or other property of such plan, or has any authority or responsibility to do so.

ERISA §3(38): This section of ERISA defines an "investment manager" as any fiduciary (other than a trustee or named fiduciary) who has the power to manage, acquire, or dispose of any plan asset, is a registered investment adviser (RIA) under the Investment Advisers Act of 1940, a bank or an insurance company, and has acknowledged in writing that he or she is a fiduciary with respect to the plan.

ERISA §405(d)(1): This section of ERISA relieves a plan fiduciary from any liability for the acts or omissions of a prudently appointed ERISA §3(38) investment manager.

ERISA Attorney: An attorney who specializes in ERISA law and can help a plan sponsor by designing and drafting plans, providing guidance to help clients understand how their plans work, advising them of changes in the law that affect their plan design or operation, and negotiating with the Internal Revenue Service, Department of Labor and Pension Benefit Guaranty Corporation, when necessary, to resolve problems.

Expense Ratio: The annual fee charged by a mutual fund for investment management services. This fee is explicitly disclosed to investors in the fund prospectus or fact sheet and automatically deducted from participant accounts.

Explicit Fees: Flat rate charges for services provided to a plan that are fully disclosed and either billed directly to the plan sponsor or to plan participants.

Fee Caps: A limit on fees charged by a service provider for certain services once plan assets reach a certain size.

Fee Disclosure: The acknowledgment by a service provider of the fees charged for the services provided to a retirement plan.

Fiduciary: A person is a fiduciary with respect to a plan to the extent (1) he exercises any discretionary authority or discretionary control respecting management of such plan or exercises any authority or control respecting management or disposition of its assets, (2) has any discretionary authority or discretionary responsibility in the administration of such plan, or (3) renders investment advice for a fee or other compensation, direct or indirect, with respect to any moneys or other property of such plan, or has any authority or responsibility to do so. See "ERISA §3(21)".

Fiduciary Audit File: A central file where information and documents relating to a retirement plan are stored for fiduciary documentation purposes.

Financial Industry Regulatory Authority (FINRA): The largest non-governmental regulator for securities firms doing business in the United States. FINRA oversees and regulates brokerage firms, brokers and registered representatives. FINRA does not regulate Registered Investment

Advisors (RIAs). FINRA was created through the consolidation of NASD and the member regulation, enforcement and arbitration functions of the New York Stock Exchange.

Flat Fee: A fully disclosed, non-asset based fee for certain services provided to a retirement plan.

Front-Loaded: An up-front commission paid to a broker, usually by an insurance company for selling a variable group annuity to a plan sponsor. These types of commissions generally result in back-end charges being assessed if the plan sponsor terminates the contract within a specified period of time.

Functional Fiduciaries: Determined by examining the role a person plays for a plan, the types of services they provide, or the discretion or control they have. Because the role is based on actions, it is possible for a person to be a fiduciary without realizing it and without knowing the duties or the consequences of not performing those duties.

Fund Sponsor: A mutual fund company.

Group Annuity: A 401k plan provided by an insurance company that bundles services together including recordkeeping, administration, investment and participant education/enrollment. A group annuity is an insurance contract and may include surrender changes if the plan sponsor terminates the contract within a specified period.

Hard Dollars: See "Explicit Fees".

Implicit Fees: See "Asset-Based Fees".

Index Funds: A mutual fund designed to match or track a broad market index such as the S&P 500. Index funds provide broad market exposure, low operating expenses, and low portfolio turnover.

Indirect Compensation: Any compensation received by a service provider that does not come directly from the plan or from participants. Examples include 12b-1 fees and sub-TA fees.

Investment Advice: Under Department of Labor (DOL) regulations, a person provides fiduciary investment advice when (1) he makes recommendations regarding the purchase or sale of securities and (2) the advice is individualized, based on the particular needs of the plan (or, in the case of participant level investment advice, on the particular needs of a participant).

Investment Advisers Act of 1940: The federal law created to regulate the actions of Registered Investment Advisors (RIAs). Investment advisors are regulated by the Securities and Exchange Commission (SEC) or a State regulatory authority.

Investment Advisory Fees: These fees are usually charged by a Registered Investment Advisor (RIA) who provides investment advice to a plan.

Investment Company Act of 1940: The federal law that was created to clearly define the responsibilities and limitations placed upon mutual fund companies that offer investment products to the public. Investment companies are regulated by the Securities and Exchange Commission (SEC).

Investment Manager: Defined by ERISA §3(38) as any fiduciary (other than a trustee or named fiduciary) who has the power to manage, acquire, or dispose of any plan asset, is a registered investment adviser (RIA) under the Investment Advisers Act of 1940, a bank or an insurance company, and has acknowledged in writing that he or she is a fiduciary with respect to the plan.

Investment Policy: The general investment goals and objectives for a plan and the strategies to meet these objectives. Specific information on matters such as asset allocation, risk tolerance, liquidity requirements, and monitoring criteria would generally be included.

Investment Policy Statement (IPS): A written document that codifies an investment policy.

Lifecycle Fund: See "Target Retirement Date Fund".

Lifestyle Fund: A single mutual fund that qualifies as a Qualified Default Investment Alternative (QDIA) under the Pension Protection Act of 2006 and features an asset mix determined by the level of risk and return that is appropriate for an individual participant. Factors that determine this mix include an investor's age, level of risk aversion, the investment's purpose and the length of time until the principal will be withdrawn. Lifestyle funds generally feature conservative, moderate, or aggressive growth strategies and are designed to be the main investment in a participant's portfolio.

Market Timing: The strategy of making buy or sell decisions about securities by attempting to predict future market price movements.

Ministerial: Non-fiduciary functions performed by a Third-Party Administrator such as determination of eligibility for plan participation, calculation of service and compensation to determine benefits, preparation of employee communications, maintenance of employment records, and preparation of reports for filing such as Form 5500.

Money Manager: A professional investment firm.

Mortality Risk and Administrative Expense (M&E Fee): A fee charged by an insurance company to cover the cost of the insurance features of an annuity contract, including the guarantee of a lifetime income payment, interest and expense guarantees, and any death benefit provided during the accumulation period.

Mutual Fund Company: An investment firm that provides mutual funds.

Mutual Fund: A professionally-managed portfolio that pools money from many investors and invests it in stocks, bonds, short-term money market instruments, and/or other securities. Mutual funds are registered with the SEC under the Investment Company Act of 1940.

Named Fiduciary: One or more fiduciaries that jointly or severally control and manage the operation and administration of the plan. Each plan must have at least one named fiduciary and, if plan assets are held in trust, the plan must have at least one trustee. Otherwise, no limits apply for the number of fiduciaries a plan may have.

National Association of Securities Dealers or (NASD): See "Financial Industry Regulatory Authority (FINRA)".

Non-Fiduciary: A service provider who does not acknowledge fiduciary status or meet the requirements of ERISA §3(21).

Non-Proprietary: Mutual funds available to investors in a 401(k) plan that are not managed by the mutual fund company who provides the 401(k) plan.

Opt-In: A plan provision that requires eligible participants of a retirement plan to affirmatively elect to participate.

Opt-Out: A plan provision that enables automatically enrolled participants of a retirement plan to affirmatively elect not to participate in the plan (or automatic deferral increases).

Participant-Directed Plan: A retirement plan that allows participants to direct their own investments.

Party in Interest: A fiduciary; a service provider; an employer any of whose employees are covered by the plan; an employee organization whose members are covered by the plan; a 50 percent or more owner of such employer or employee organization; a spouse, ancestor, lineal descendent, or spouse of a lineal descendant of any of the persons above except an employee organization; a corporation, partnership, trust or estate of which 50 percent is owned directly or indirectly by persons above (other than relatives); an employee, officer, director or 10 percent or more shareholder of any of the persons mentioned above except a fiduciary or a relative; and, a 10 percent or more partner or joint venture of any person above except a fiduciary or relative.

Passive Management: Passive management is most often characterized by index funds and Exchange-Traded Funds (ETFs) which attempt to replicate broad market indexes by purchasing the securities that compose them. The goal is to attempt to match market index returns rather than achieve better-than-market returns. Passive strategies generally provide broad market exposure, low operating expenses, and low portfolio turnover.

Pay to Play: (1) A mutual fund company (or insurance company) who requires another mutual fund company to share revenue in order to be accessible in the first fund company's retirement plan product. (2) The misuse of Section 28(e) fees or "soft dollars" by a mutual fund to garner the loyalty of retirement plan consultants.

Pension: See "Defined Benefit Plan".

Pension Protection Act of 2006 (PPA): Signed into law on August 17, 2006, it represents the most sweeping pension legislation in over 30 years and includes a number of significant tax incentives to enhance and protect retirement savings for millions of Americans.

Per Participant Fee: A fee that is usually charged by a TPA for administration services.

Plan Administrator: The plan administrator, as defined by ERISA §3(16)(A), is the person specifically designated in the plan document or in most cases, the plan sponsor. The plan administrator oversees the operation of the plan. See "ERISA §3(16)".

Plan Document: The plan document enables the plan administrator to determine who is eligible to be in the plan, when eligible employees enter the plan, what benefits are available, how contributions are made to the plan (i.e., employer contributions, employee contributions, or both), how and when the benefits are paid, and how claim disputes are resolved.

Plan Trustee: ERISA requires plan assets to be held in trust by one or more trustees. The trustees must either be named in the written documents or be appointed by a named fiduciary. The trustee(s) has the exclusive authority to manage and control the assets of the plan.

Portfolio: An appropriate mix of or collection of investments.

Professionally Managed Account: A type of Qualified Default Investment Alternative (QDIA) whereby an ERISA §3(38) investment manager manages participant accounts or managed portfolios on a discretionary basis.

Profit-Sharing Plan: A retirement plan in which the contributions are made solely by the employer via one of several allocation methods.

Prohibited Transactions: Five categories of ERISA-specified actions that a fiduciary may not cause the plan to engage in, directly or indirectly, with a party in interest.

Proprietary Mutual Fund: A mutual fund that is managed by a fund company that also provides retirement plan services. Fund companies face conflicts of interest when they recommend their own funds over that of another provider to retirement plan clients.

Prudent Man Rule: The standard under which the ERISA fiduciary must act. The fiduciary is required to act "with the care, skill, prudence, and diligence under the circumstances then prevailing that a prudent man acting in a like capacity and familiar with such matters would use in the conduct of an enterprise of a like character and with like aims."

Qualified Default Investment Alternatives (QDIAs): Under the Pension Protection Act of 2006, an age-based, life cycle or targeted-retirement-date fund or account, a risk-based balanced fund and/or a managed account that provides long-term appreciation and capital preservation through a mix of equity and fixed income exposures. A QDIA must be managed by an investment manager or an investment company registered under the Investment Company Act of 1940.

Record-keeper: Record-keepers are responsible for keeping track of participant account activity and balances. Services may include processing investment transactions, maintaining a participant and plan sponsor website, handling participant requests for loans or hardship withdrawals and providing participant and plan sponsor reports, enrollment kits, etc.

Registered Investment Adviser (RIA): An advisor, registered with the Securities and Exchange Commission (SEC) or State regulatory authority, which manages the investments of others and is able to provide investment advice for a fee. RIAs are governed by the Investment Advisors Act of 1940 and usually serve in a fiduciary capacity.

Retail vs. Institutional Pricing: Mutual funds often have two flavors of the same fund. Retail mutual funds are typically sold by brokers and registered representatives to retail investors and carry higher expense ratios. Institutional versions of mutual funds are lower cost and typically utilized by select firms such as Registered Investment Advisors (RIAs) and sometimes require high investment minimums (i.e. $1 million).

Retainer: A fixed annual fee charged by a service provider that entitles the plan sponsor to certain scope of services.

Revenue Sharing: The arrangement where a mutual fund shares part of its revenue with other service providers to offset or underwrite other plan services such as recordkeeping and administration. Also known as Sub-TA fees.

 Sales Charge: A commission charged by a mutual fund at the time of purchase to compensate the selling broker.

Sales Load: See "Sales Charges".

Section 28(e) Fees ("Soft Dollars"): Payments that occur between investment companies (i.e. mutual funds) and their service providers, pursuant to SEC rule 28(e). While these payments are legal, SEC investigations have shown that soft dollars have often been used by mutual fund companies to buy the loyalty of consultants.

Securities and Exchange Commission (SEC): The Federal agency responsible for administering federal securities laws in the US.

Series 6: The securities license entitling the holder to sell mutual funds and variable annuities.

Series 63: A securities license entitling the holder to solicit orders for any type of security in a particular state.

Series 65: A securities license required by most U.S. states entitling the holder to act as an investment advisor and to provide investment advice for a fee.

Series 7: A securities license entitling the holder to sell all types of corporate securities, except commodities and futures.

Share Class: Many mutual fund companies have created different classes of shares for their mutual funds which have different fee schedules associated with them. These different share classes typically provide additional amounts of compensation and revenue sharing to brokers and TPAs.

Statement of Additional Information (SAI): A supplementary document to a mutual fund's prospectus that contains additional information about the fund and includes further disclosure regarding its operations.

Sub-Accounts: Group annuity investment options that are similar to mutual funds in look and feel. They often carry the same name and are operated by the same companies as publicly offered mutual funds but they are not the same. Sub-accounts usually have a different and higher expense structure than their mutual fund counterparts, and possibly a far different return.

Sub-Transfer Agent fees (or Sub-TA fees): See "Revenue Sharing".

Surrender Charge: An early redemption fee sometimes charged by an insurance company with a group annuity contract that is assessed if the plan terminates its contract within a specified period of time.

Target Retirement-Date Fund: A single mutual fund that qualifies as a Qualified Default Investment Alternative (QDIA) under the Pension Protection Act of 2006 and ties the asset allocation of the portfolio to a specific retirement date. For instance, a 2030 fund would generally be suitable for a participant who expects to retire in 2030. These funds are meant to be the main investment in a participant's portfolio and automatically adjust the asset allocation, becoming more conservative, as the participant approaches retirement.

Third-Party Administrator (TPA): A company that may provide consulting services such as plan design and reporting, administration and recordkeeping, process contributions, generate statements, complete IRS required annual filings, and perform non-discrimination testing. Also known as a "contract administrator".

Trading Costs: Costs incurred by a mutual fund each time it buys or sells securities within the portfolio. These costs (such as commissions, bid/ask spreads, market impact, etc.) serve to reduce investor returns.

Trailing Commission: See "12b-1 fee".

Transfer Agent: Typically a bank, trust company, or mutual fund that provides services such as shareholder recordkeeping, trade execution, or order settlement.

Trustee-Directed Plan: A plan where decisions are directed by the plan trustees rather than the plan participants.

Turnover: The buying and selling of securities within a portfolio (i.e. mutual fund). For instance, a fund with 100 percent turnover buys and sells the entire portfolio in a given year while a fund with 200 percent turnover buys and sells the entire portfolio twice in a given year.

Unbundled: A retirement plan where the recordkeeping, administration, investment, and education services are provided by multiple companies.

Wrap Fee: An inclusive fee, generally found in group annuity insurance contracts, that is based on a percentage of plan assets. This fee covers the costs associated with a retirement plan such as recordkeeping, administration and marketing. The wrap fee is in addition to any investment related fees charged by the sub-accounts.

Notes

Chapter 1 - The 401(k) Industry Is Broken!

1. ERISA §404(a)(1)(B).

Chapter 2 - Focusing on Successful Outcomes

1. Olga Sorokina, Anthony Webb, and Dan Muldoon, *Pension Wealth and Income: 1992, 1998, and 2004* (Center for Retirement Research at Boston College, 2008).

Chapter 3 - Understanding Fiduciary Responsibility

1. ERISA §409.
2. ERISA §404(a)(1)(A).
3. U.S. Department of Labor "A Look at 401(k) Plan Fees.", Publications, 3.
4. *Brussian vs. RJR Nabisco.* (5th Circuit Court, 2000).
5. ERISA §404(a)(1)(B).
6. ERISA §404(a)(1)(C).
7. ERISA §404(a)(1)(D).
8. ERISA §406 (a)(1).
9. Fred Reish, "Just Out of Reish: Menu Monitors."

September 2005. http://www.plansponsor.com/magazine_type1/?RECORD_ID=30735 (accessed February 25, 2008).

10. W. Scott Simon, "Fiduciary Focus: Non-Fiduciary Investment Consultants" May 4, 2006. http://advisor.morningstar.com/articles/doc.asp?s=1&docId=4432 (accessed March 24, 2008).
11. Ibid.
12. Pete Swisher, *401(k) Fiduciary Governance: An Advisor's Guide* (Arlington, VA: ASPPA, 2008).
13. ERISA §3(21)(A)(2).
14. ERISA §405(d)(1).
15. Swisher, *401(k) Fiduciary, 306.*
16. Fred Reish, "Participant Investing: Forewarned is Forearmed" September 2004. http://www.reish.com/publications/article_detail.cfm?ARTICLEID=475 (accessed April 6, 2008).
17. Swisher, *401(k) Fiduciary, 18.*
18. Center for Fiduciary Studies.

Chapter 4 - Understanding the Players

1. Fred Reish, "Just Out of Reish: Menu Monitors" September 2005. http://www.plansponsor.com/magazine_type1/?RECORD_ID=30735 (accessed February 25, 2008).

Chapter 5 - Protecting Participants from Themselves

1. Portions of this chapter originally appeared in "$450,000 Per Participant...The Value of An Independent Fiduciary" by Joshua P. Itzoe and Matthew

D. Hutcheson and can be found at www.greenspringwealth.com.

2. The Burgess study was a commissioned study by John Hancock. The study examined the performance of 14,487 retirement plan participants from 1997-2006 contributing to their employer's defined contribution plans through an ARA group annuity contract issued by John Hancock USA. The Lifestyle group (i.e., professionally managed approach) represents those participants that invested only in a single Lifestyle Portfolio throughout the period. The Non-Lifestyle group (i.e., do-it-yourselfers) represents those participants who chose their own portfolio mix throughout the period. Burgess & Associates and John Hancock USA are not affiliated.

3. DALBAR. "Quantitative Analysis of Investor Behavior." 2007.

4. W. Scott Simon, "Fiduciary Focus: Non-Fiduciary Investment Consultants." May 4, 2006. http://advisor.morningstar.com/articles/doc.asp?s=1&docId=4432 (accessed March 24, 2008).

5. Jeffrey C. Chang, , W. Scott Simon, and Gary K. Allen, "A Step Beyond ERISA Section 404(c): Improving on the Participant-Directed 401(k) Investment Model." *Journal of Pension Benefits* 12 , no. 4 (Summer 2005): 5-12.

6. George Chimento, "A Victory for Participants. A Warning Shot for Plan Sponsors." February 20, 2008. http://www.theworkplace.biz/LaRue_article_nf.html (accessed February 26, 2008).

7. Brooks Hamilton, interview by Hendrick Smith. *Frontline*.PBS. (February 23, 2006).

Chapter 6 - Deciphering Fees & Expenses

1. U.S. Department of Labor, "A Look at 401(k) Plan Fees." Publications, 3.
2. Matthew D. Hutcheson, , interview by Rick Meigs. An Interview with Matthew D. Hutcheson, Recent Congressional Witness on 401k Fees (2007).
3. Statement by David Certner, Legislative Counsel and Legislative Policy Director of AARP: "Even a difference of only 50 basis points, from 0.5 percent to 1.0 percent, would reduce the value of the account by $17,417, or a little over 13 percent over the 30-year period."
4. 1999 DOL Model Fee Disclosure
5. Matthew Gnabasik, "Monitoring 401(k) Plan Cost." In *The 401(k) Plan Sponsor's Fiduciary Toolkit (2nd Edition)*. (Portland, OR, 2005). Gnabasik asserts that "According to Spectrem Group's projections, the aggregate 401(k) marketplace generates $13.204 billion of total fees, of which 89.5 percent ($11.817 billion) is derived from asset fees, while the remaining 10.5 percent ($1.387 billion) comes from service fees." These statistics can be found in "Plan Sponsors Need Better Fix on 401(k) Fees," *Employee Benefit Plan Review*, September 2001, p. 22.
6. Matthew Gnabasik, "Monitoring 401(k) Plan Cost." In *The 401(k) Plan Sponsor's Fiduciary Toolkit (2nd Edition)*.
7. Transfer Agents. http://www.sec.gov/answers/transferagent.htm (accessed April 6, 2008).
8. Administration, Pension and Welfare Benefits. "Study of 401(k) Plan Fees and Expenses." April 13, 1998.

9. Tim Middleton, "Annuities Load 401(k)s with Fees." September 28, 2004. http://moneycentral.msn.com/content/P94081.asp (accessed April 6, 2008).
10. Center for Fiduciary Studies. "Guide to SEC Probe of Consultant Pay-to-Play Schemes." January 16, 2004.
11. Gnabasik, "Monitoring 401(k) Plan Cost." In *The 401(k) Plan Sponsor's Fiduciary Toolkit (2nd Edition).*
12. Ibid.
13. DOL Advisory Opinion 2001-01A.
14. Swisher, *401(k) Fiduciary Governance*, 488-489.
15. Ibid.

Chapter 7 - Tips for Containing Plan Costs

1. The Investment Company Institute. "The US Retirement Market." 2006.
2. Pete Swisher, "Fiduciary Governance of a Qualified Plan." *The ASPPA Journal* (Winter 2008).

Chapter 8 - PPA and Successful Plan Design

1. U.S. Department of Labor. "Regulation Relating To Qualified Default Investment Alternatives In Participant-Directed Individual Account Plans." http://www.dol.gov/ebsa/newsroom/fsQDIA.html (accessed April 6, 2008).
2. Ibid.

Chapter 9 - Developing an Investment Policy

1. Dimensional Fund Advisors study (2002) of 44 In-

stitutional equity pension plans with $452 billion of total assets.

2. ERISA §402(b)(1).

Chapter 10 - Choosing Active vs. Passive Investments

1. Mark Carhart, "Persistence in Mutual Fund Performance." *Journal of Finance* (March 1997): 57-82.
2. Laura Bruce, "Mutual Fund Turnover and Taxes." November 6, 2003. http://www.bankrate.com/brm/news/investing/20020306a.asp (accessed February 23, 2008).
3. Matthew D. Hutcheson, "Uncovering and Understanding Hidden Fees in Qualified Retirement Plans." *The Elder Law Journal* 15, no. 2 (Fall 2007). http://www.401khelpcenter.com/pdf/mdh_understanding_fees_v4.pdf (accessed March 25, 2008).
4. "Dead Funds and Return of Surviving Mutual Funds Relative to the Market, 1970-2000 (31 years)-CRSP."

Chapter 11 - The Ideal 401(k) Plan

1. Gregory Kasten, *Retirement Success: A Complete Instruction Guide For Plan Sponsors & Their Advisors.* (United Trust Company, 536.)
2. HR Investment Consultants. *401k Averages Book, 8th Edition.* (HR Investment Consultants, 14.)

Chapter 12 - A Case Study

1. The EBRI/ICI 401(k) database, the largest database of 401(k) plan participant accounts, showed that the median account balance was $66,650 at year-end 2006.

2. Estimated immediate fixed-income annuity quote available from www.fidelity.com (as of 3-25-2008). The quote assumes a 65-year old Maryland resident, male. Guarantees are subject to the claims-paying ability of the issuing insurance company.

3. Ibid.

Bibliography

Administration, Pension and Welfare Benefits. "Study of 401(k) Plan Fees and Expenses." April 13, 1998.

Bruce, Laura. "Mutual Fund Turnover and Taxes." November 6, 2003. http://www.bankrate.com/brm/news/investing/20020306a.asp (accessed February 23, 2008).

Brussian vs. RJR Nabisco. (5th Circuit Court, 2000).

Carhart, Mark. "Persistence in Mutual Fund Performance." *Journal of Finance* (March 1997): 57-82.

Center for Fiduciary Studies. "Guide to SEC Probe of Consultant Pay-to-Play Schemes." January 16, 2004.

Certner, David. Testimony Before The House Ways And Means Committee On The Appropriateness Of Retirement Plan Fees, Washington, D.C., (October 30, 2007).

Chang, Jeffrey C., W. Scott Simon, and Gary K. Allen. "A Step Beyond ERISA Section 404(c): Improving on the Participant-Directed 401(k) Investment Model." *Journal of Pension Benefits* 12, no. 4 (Summer 2005): 5-12.

Chimento, George L. "A Victory for Participants. A Warning Shot for Plan Sponsors." February 20, 2008. http://www.theworkplace.biz/LaRue_article_nf.html (accessed February 26, 2008).

DALBAR. "Quantitative Analysis of Investor Behavior." 2007.

"Dead Funds and Return of Surviving Mutual Funds Relative to the Market, 1970-2000 (31 years)- CRSP."

DOL Advisory Opinion 2001-01A.

Gnabasik, Matthew. "Monitoring 401(k) Plan Cost." In The 401(k) Plan Sponsor's Fiduciary Toolkit (2nd Edition). Portland, OR: the 401khelpcenter.com, 2005.

Hamilton, Brooks, interview by Hendrick Smith. Frontline, PBS (February 23, 2006).

HR Investment Consultants. 401k Averages Book, 8th Edition. Baltimore, MD: HR Investment Consultants, 2007.

Hutcheson, Matthew D., interview by Rick Meigs. An Interview with Matthew D. Hutcheson, Recent Congressional Witness on 401k Fees (2007). http://www.401khelpcenter.com/401k/meigs_mdh_interview.html (accessed March 25, 2008)

Hutcheson, Matthew D. "Uncovering and Understanding Hidden Fees in Qualified Retirement Plans." *The Elder Law Journal* 15, no. 2 (Fall 2007).

The Investment Company Institute. "The US Retirement Market." 2006.

Kasten, Gregory. *Retirement Success: A Complete Instruction Guide For Plan Sponsors & Their Advisors.* Lexington, KY: Unified Trust Company, 2004.

http://www.dol.gov/ebsa/newsroom/fsQDIA.html (accessed April 6, 2008).

Middleton, Tim. "Annuities Load 401(k)s with Fees." September 28, 2004. http://moneycentral.msn.com/content/P94081.asp (accessed April 6, 2008).

"Plan Sponsors Need Better Fix on 401(k) Fees." *Employee Benefit Plan Review* (September 2001): 22.

Reish, Fred. "Just Out of Reish: Menu Monitors." September 2005. http://www.plansponsor.com/magazine_type1/?RECORD_ID=30735 (accessed February 25, 2008).

"Participant Investing: Forewarned is Forearmed." September 2004. http://www.reish.com/publications/article_detail.cfm?ARTICLEID=475 (accessed April 6, 2008).

Simon, W. Scott. "Fiduciary Focus: Non-Fiduciary Investment Consultants." May 4, 2006. http://advisor.morningstar.com/articles/doc.asp?s=1&docId=4432 (accessed March 24, 2008).

Sorokina, Olga, Anthony Webb, and Dan Muldoon. *Pension Wealth and Income: 1992, 1998, and 2004.* Center for Retirement Research at Boston College (CRR), 2008.

Swisher, Pete. *401(k) Fiduciary Governance: An Advisor's Guide.* Arlington, VA: ASPPA, 2008.

"Fiduciary Governance of a Qualified Plan." *The ASPPA Journal* (Winter 2008):13-20.

Transfer Agents. http://www.sec.gov/answers/transferagent.htm (accessed April 6, 2008).

U.S. Department of Labor. "Regulation Relating To Qualified Default Investment Alternatives In Participant-Directed Individual Account Plans."

"A Look at 401(k) Plan Fees."

Author Biography

Joshua P. Itzoe, CFP®, AIF® is a Principal of Greenspring Wealth Management, a registered investment advisory firm and Independent Fiduciary in Towson, MD. He leads the firm's institutional advisory practice which provides fiduciary governance consulting and ERISA §3(38) services to plans that generally range between $5 million and $100 million. Itzoe has written articles pertaining to fiduciary responsibility for *Benefits & Compensation Digest* and *Employee Benefit News* and has also been quoted extensively in such publications as *SmartMoney Magazine, Kiplinger's Retirement Report, The Baltimore Examiner, Journal of Financial Planning, Investment Advisor, Registered Rep, Planadviser Magazine, Financial Advisor* and *National Underwriter Life and Health.* He has served as an Instructor for the Community College of Baltimore County (CCBC) in the area of financial planning and was selected as one of "America's Top Financial Planners" for 2008 by the Consumers' Research Council of America. Itzoe graduated with honors from Wake Forest University with a Bachelor of Arts degree and is a CERTIFIED FINANCIAL PLANNER™ and Accredited Investment Fiduciary®.

To learn more, please visit **www.fixingthe401k.com** or **www.greenspringwealth.com.**

CPSIA information can be obtained
at www.ICGtesting.com
Printed in the USA
FSHW01n0711180518
48402FS